THE COMMONWEALTH AND INTERNATIONAL LIBRARY

Joint Chairmen of the Honorary Editorial Advisory Board
SIR ROBERT ROBINSON, O.M., F.R.S., LONDON
DEAN ATHELSTAN SPILHAUS, MINNESOTA

Publisher : ROBERT MAXWELL, M.C., M.P.

SOCIETY, SCHOOLS AND PROGRESS

General Editor : DR. E. J. KING

SOCIETY, SCHOOLS AND PROGRESS IN NIGERIA

SOCIETY, SCHOOLS AND PROGRESS IN NIGERIA

BY

L. J. LEWIS

Institute of Education, University of London

PERGAMON PRESS

OXFORD · LONDON · EDINBURGH · NEW YORK
PARIS · FRANKFURT

PERGAMON PRESS LTD.
Headington Hill Hall, Oxford
4 & 5 Fitzroy Square, London W.1

PERGAMON PRESS (SCOTLAND) LTD.
2 & 3 Teviot Place, Edinburgh 1

PERGAMON PRESS INC.
122 East 55th Street, New York 22, N.Y.

PERGAMON PRESS GmbH
Kaiserstrasse 75, Frankfurt-am-Main

FEDERAL PUBLICATIONS LTD.
Times House, River Valley Rd., Singapore

SAMCAX BOOK SERVICES LTD.
Queensway, P.O. Box 2720, Nairobi, Kenya

First edition 1965

Library of Congress Catalog Card No. 65–23938

*Set in 10 on 12 pt. Baskerville
and printed in Great Britain by Watmoughs Limited of Bradford*

COMPARATIVE STUDIES

An Introduction to the Series "Society, Schools and Progress"

By Edmund King

This volume is one of a mutually supporting series of books on SOCIETY, SCHOOLS AND PROGRESS in a number of important countries or regions. The series is intended to serve students of sociology, government and politics, as well as education. Investment in education, or satisfaction of the consumer demand for it, is now the biggest single item of non-military public expenditure in many countries and an increasing proportion in all the rest. The systematic use of education to achieve security, prosperity and social well-being makes it imperative to have up-to-date surveys realistically related to all these objectives; for it is impossible to study one effectively without reference to the others or to assess the objectives without reference to education as the chosen instrument.

Comparative studies of all kinds are in vogue. We find university departments of comparative government, law, religion, anthropology, literature and the like. Some comparison is taken for granted in a contracting world of closer relationships. But not all comparative studies are forward-looking or constructive. Comparisons based solely or mainly on backward-looking interests can have their own kind of respectability without necessarily drawing lessons for the present. However, some contemporary comparisons show utility as well as interest or respectability, particularly when observers are enabled to analyse social organization, formative customs, value system and so forth.

More important still are area studies based upon a comprehensive survey of a whole culture, showing the interpenetration of its technology, government, social relationships, religion and arts; for here we see our neighbours making man—and making him in an idiom which challenges our own assumptions and practices. This concerted and conscious making of posterity by a multiplicity of interlocking influences is perhaps mankind's most astonishing feature—at least on a par with rationality and speech, and inseparable from them. As the last third of the twentieth century begins, however, we are witnessing the struggle of competing educational prescriptions for the whole future of mankind.

THE MAKING OF THE FUTURE

The most important studies of all in the world today are those undertaken with a view to modifying deliberately the formative conditions in which our children and their descendants will live —that is to say, their education. In the pre-industrial past there was plenty of time for the slow evolution of civilization and technology. Even in this century people used to think of societies and education as growing empirically and evolving. Today's world cannot wait upon the spontaneity that sufficed yesterday. It is often said that the Industrial Revolution is entering on its second and more important phase—the systematic application to *social* relationships of mechanized and urban-style abundance, with a corresponding transformation of all learning opportunities.

Certainly that is the dream of the hitherto underprivileged majority of mankind. All countries are involved in this social stocktaking and reckoning for the future, no matter whether they are called socialistic or capitalistic. In any case, the pace of change is so fast everywhere that some co-ordination or phasing of development is accepted as a critical responsibility of statecraft in all countries.

THE TRANSFORMATION OF EDUCATION

In relation to education, this sequence of events has already been attended by remarkable changes. Education used to be undertaken largely at home, by society at large, by working relationships or by voluntary organizations. Now it is a publicly regulated, publicly financed activity for the most part. It is provided as a necessary service by an expanding range of public employees. Of course unofficial people and social groups continue to take a keen interest, especially in their own children; but increasingly it is the State which co-ordinates and directs the process for all children. In some countries the State claims a monopoly of education; in most others that claim is hotly resisted, though inevitably the State is conceded a growing share in the partnership.

In any case, the State or its professional subsidiaries will assume a mounting responsibility for the allocation of funds, for increasingly expensive instruments and premises, for ensuring fair distribution of opportunity, for preventing the waste of talent, for safeguarding economic and social well-being and for setting the national priorities into proper order. Therefore, no matter what education has been in the past, the logic of the Industrial Revolution has turned it into publicly regulated and publicly provided activities, directed towards the deliberate construction of a more satisfactory future.

That commitment is now implicitly indivisible within any one country. It is also accepted that internationally, too, everyone's education is likely to be to the advantage of everyone else in the long run. For this reason alone, international comparisons and assessments are of the utmost importance.

Whole countries are finding that their external context is changing in unprecedented ways. The emancipation of formerly subject peoples is a conspicuous example. Another instance is seen in the large regional developments whereby food production, commerce, and mutual protection are ensured in "developing countries"—usually with some notable reliance on educational improvements. Even quite powerful and well-established countries (like several in Western Europe) co-operate increasingly with their neighbours for commercial and political reasons; and all these changes necessitate some adjustment of school orientation and programmes, if only for the interchange of personnel. Apart from such specific instances, it is increasingly obvious that no education anywhere is worth the name unless it is viable in world terms.

Great though these adjustments are between sovereign nations, the changes that transcend all national boundaries and apply to all school systems alike are even more radically influential. In all countries, the area of education monopolized by the schools and other formally instructive institutions is diminishing in relation to educative forces outside. For example, the first public television programmes in the world began in 1936; yet within twenty-five years television and radio absorbed almost as much of children's time and interest (taking the year all round) as the formal school hours in a number of countries. The appeal of such external influences may be greater than the schools'. The universal teacher problem accentuates the change.

In any case, all instruction offered in school is largely conditional for its success on subsequent reinforcement. This it does not always get in a world of expanding opportunities and experiences for young people, which challenge schools' previous prerogatives and sometimes their precepts. A whole new range of "service occupations" provides alternative perspectives. Furthermore, technological and social change necessitate much professional retraining and personal reorientation in all advanced countries. There is far less idea of a once-for-all preparation for life. Learning the unknown is taking the place of teaching the certainties.

In all countries we share this uncertainty. Deeply rooted though we all are in our own ways of life, our scrutiny of the future becomes increasingly a comparison of our hypotheses and experiments. No really adequate answers to any educational or social problem can be determined within one country's confines any longer. Comparative Education is above all the discipline which systematizes our observations and conclusions in relation to the shaping of the future.

COMPARATIVE EDUCATION IN GENERAL

Comparative studies of education are necessarily based upon existing practices, institutions, and background influences which have shaped the present variety of educational idioms throughout the world. It is essential to acquaint ourselves with the most important systems, not as alien phenomena but as variations upon the preoccupations of every family and every school in our own country. To be both civilized and scientific we must try to "feel inside" the common human concerns of our neighbours. By this transference of sympathy we achieve some sort of detachment which will enable us to appreciate our own involvement in circumstances—quite as much as theirs.

What adds up to education in our own country is as confused a tangle as any to be found in those other countries where we more easily assume the role of critical advisers. Much of it is habituation, and much is emotionally bound rather than rational. Advice and rational planning that do not take account of these actual influences on education at any one place and time are unscientific as well as failing in humanity. From a practical point of view, too, they will fail, because they lack a sense of the local and topical dynamic. We must know the living present. It is this that gives momentum to the future and conditions it. Thus, even at this first or informative stage of Comparative Education, we are made analytically aware (not only descriptively) of today's climax of forces. We inevitably envisage some possibilities for the future—if only with reference to our own reactions and purposes.

Therefore, though Comparative Education must go on to study particular problems (such as control or university expansion), it must begin with area studies or dynamic analyses of concurrent influences such as this series provides. Without awareness of what "education" seems now to be to its participants, no student or planner can effectively share in the shaping of the future. He may have falsely identified his "problems". He will probably misjudge their topical significance. On the basis of unrealistic generalizations he will certainly fail to communicate acceptable advice. The climax of local culture which amounts to education in any one place is emotionally more sensitive even than language issues or religion, because it includes within itself these very influences and many others.

THE PURPOSE OF THIS SERIES

SOCIETY, SCHOOLS AND PROGRESS are here surveyed in the world's most significant countries—significant not simply for reasons of technological or political strength, but because of the widely relevant decisions in education now being taken. Since the end of the Second World War a ferment of reform has been going on. No reform takes place in the sterile conditions of a laboratory. In the social field not even research can be isolated and sterilized. Experiment in education involves all the untidiness and unpredictability of human responses, which are the source of all creative ingenuity. Every planner or theorist, every student of "problems" that seem abstract and general enough, needs an opportunity of studying again and again the forensic application of his theories.

Nevertheless, so that some general study may be made of frequently recurring tendencies and problems, the books in the SOCIETY, SCHOOLS AND PROGRESS series are arranged in a fairly uniform pattern. They all begin with the historical and institutional background. They then go on to describe administration, the school system, family influences, and background social forces in much the same order of progression. Thus it is easy to make cross-references from one volume to another. Cross-cultural analysis of particular problems or interests is facilitated, but always in relation to the living context which so often reveals unexpected pitfalls or opportunities.

After this second or "problem" level of cross-cultural analysis in detail, the serious student can go on to a third stage. He can assess as a dynamic whole the collective preparation for the future of each of the countries featured. This third level of assessing orientation, or of planning, is not always marked by logic alone within any one of the countries concerned; but an international survey of discernible trends can be of great practical importance. The evolving form of the future can at least be surmised, and continuing research can guide it.

Public investment in education (and consumer demand still more) has often been a precarious venture from the half-known into the unsuspected. Yet buildings, teachers and the children's lives may be committed for generations. For this third level of comparative analysis it is therefore necessary to work closely with specialists in other disciplines, such as economists and sociologists. But the specialist in Comparative Education gives insight and information to them, just as he receives from them. Making the future is no project for any one man, any one discipline, any one interpretation.

This brings us to a last general point. It is more important than ever to have soundly based comparative studies of education, because the relevance of even the best of systems has limits imposed by time. Reorientation and retraining successively throughout life will be the experience of most people in advanced countries for generations to come. That trend is already evident at the most educated levels in the United States, Sweden, Britain and some other countries. All human roles are being transformed, too, not just subjects and occupations. Therefore it is useless to rely on what has been done, or is being done, in schools. We must try instead to think of what will be required, and to observe experiments now being undertaken on the very frontiers of education, where new matrices, new media, new elements and methods of learning are being revealed.

The less settled educational patterns of "developing countries" (where most of mankind live) make it easier for them to be radical. They can by-pass the institutions, methods and curricula of older-established school systems in their eager pursuit of unprecedented but valid objectives. This is all immediately important to us, because the whole world's educative relationships are being transformed, our own along with all the others. For that reason, one or more of the books in each batch of volumes published in the SOCIETY, SCHOOLS AND PROGRESS series will deal with a developing country, whose experience is particularly relevant in assessing education's contribution to the future.

THE PARTICULAR CASE OF NIGERIA

Nigeria makes a good field of study for obvious reasons. In the first place, all newly developing countries are of the greatest importance in any evaluation of the purposes and limitations of education as that has evolved in Western Europe and the United States. Developing countries must evidently build their future by an unprecedented use of a planned educational system, starting often from modest resources and partially co-ordinated endeavours. Some, like Nigeria, must build even nationhood out of a multiplicity of elements, and do, armed in the uncertainties of an ex-colonial experience.

Thus the experiments of Nigeria are of obvious importance far beyond her boundaries. As Africans, the Nigerians are closely scrutinized by neighbours throughout the huge continent. As men of colour, they are watched with special interest by the coloured majority of mankind. As hitherto underdeveloped people, they are helping to lead the rapid development of more than 2000 million people who have until now been in a similar position. Inevitably, therefore, their use and modification of previously unquestioned instruments of education seem likely to bring challenges (perhaps enlightenment) to educators everywhere.

CONTENTS

ACKNOWLEDGEMENTS

I wish to acknowledge the help given to me in the writing of this book through discussion and shared experience by my colleagues in the Department of Education in Tropical Areas of the University of London Institute of Education, to Miss Margaret Richards and Miss Marjorie Taylor who reduced my illegible handwriting to typescript, and to Mrs. Helen Coppen whose reading of the manuscript in draft eradicated the worst ambiguities and errors of style and structure. Much is owed to information and experiences shared with me by friends still directly engaged in education in Nigeria. Whatever defects there may be in the book I fear are my own making.

L. J. Lewis

CHAPTER I

INTRODUCTION

NIGERIA is a country in an early stage of social, political and economic modernization. On 29 March 1962 Chief Okotie-Eboh, the Federal Finance Minister of Nigeria, said in his budget speech: "I can see a vision of a new and prosperous Nigeria— a Nigeria whose blood is virile and whose aspirations are fixed by noble objectives. The sleeping giant of Africa is awake and determined to take her rightful place marching with the rest of humanity."* These words were spoken of a country of 55 million people occupying an area of 356,500 square miles, newly independent of British colonial rule, economically dependent at the present time upon a small range of primary products, but rich in potential though very far from its proclaimed goal of "a modern diversified and virtually self-sustaining (economic) system".

The position of Nigeria in relation to the rest of the world can be illustrated by comparing the standards of living expressed in money income and in units of energy consumed as is shown in the table prepared for the United Nations Conference on the application of Science and Technology for the Benefit of the Less Developed Countries held at Geneva in February 1963.† To match the income level of Italy, the lowest of the Western countries referred to, Nigeria will have to increase the income *per capita* per annum more than sixfold, and its energy consumption will need to be increased more than thirtyfold. In so doing Nigeria will reach a level of economy just a little higher than the present standards of Japan, the only non-Western nation that has succeeded in matching the technological application of the West.

* Quoted by W. F. Stolper, The development of Nigeria, *Scientific American* (New York), 209, (3) (1963), 169.

† See note on following page.

"Unfortunately, technological-induced prosperity is increasing more rapidly than, at the other end of the scale, the less developed countries can cope with their pressing necessities. And this despite the new 'social philosophy' by which, after the Second World War, Governments accepted a new responsibility, not only for their own people but for the well-being of people of other countries as well."* During the 1950's aid and investment from private and public sources, and international loans amounting to the equivalent of 30,000 million U.S. dollars were made to 100 countries and territories which can be classed as under-developed. The increase in income per person per annum in these countries after ten years was about 1 U.S. dollar.

Nigeria epitomizes the non-Western and non-industrialized countries of Africa, Asia and Latin America in respect of income and energy consumption. In other respects also, she has in common social and political factors which inhibit the organizational breakthrough for economic and social development and which are characteristic of countries similarly struggling at the poverty line of subsistence economy.

It is a country that ethnically and culturally has yet to attain

† United Nations, *Science and Technology for Development*, vol. I, *World of Opportunity* (United Nations, New York, 1963), p. 38.

Country	Population (million)	Income (equivalent U.S. dollars per annum)	Net food (calories per day)	Energy (coal-equivalent tons per annum)
U.S.A.	180·7	2289	3100	8·79
Canada	17·8	1545	3100	7·90
United Kingdom	52·5	1084	3200	5·12
Belgium	9·2	978	2900	4·27
West Germany	53·4	967	2900	4·02
Netherlands	11·5	803	3000	3·04
Italy	49·4	509	2700	1·57
Japan	93·2	341	2200	1·42
India	432·5	62	1800	0·15
Nigeria	35·1	84	—	0·05
World	2995	—	—	1·53

* *Ibid.*, p. 38.

to a national integration of its diverse peoples. This state of affairs is evidenced in the politics and government of the country. Underlying the problem of social, economic and political development is the need to develop the education system in such a way as to provide a satisfactory flow of men and women capable of acquiring the skills necessary to exploit to the fullest the natural resources of the country for the benefit of the community as a whole and to obtain the understanding co-operation of all the people in the development of the country.

Prior to embarking upon the National Development Plan for 1962–8, with the assistance of a variety of regional and international commissions, the potential resources for economic development were surveyed. Included in the resources examined was the human resource—skilled manpower. In 1776 the Scottish political economist, Adam Smith in his *magnum opus*, *The Wealth of Nations*, included in his concept of "fixed capital" "the acquired and useful abilities of all the inhabitants or members of society". In that Nigeria is among the first of the African countries to give detailed attention to this aspect of planning development, the degree of success or failure of the National Development Plan and subsequent plans will affect not only Nigeria but also the rest of Africa. In the end success will depend upon the extent to which the education system is modified and expanded to make it possible for the youth of the country to become not only technically effective but also socially effective persons. This involves much more than expansion of an educational system which at the present time is still largely imitative of the system that has grown up in the United Kingdom and reflects the characteristics of the society which it serves.

In this book an attempt is made to put the provision of education with reference to the historical, social and economic factors and in the context of a policy of development which has as its main objective the attainment of self-sustaining social and economic growth for the nation. Past estimates of priorities for development and projections of rates of growth, as in most countries, have frequently proved unsatisfactory. Improved sources of information, reflection upon past experience and disciplined determination to maintain effort along directly productive lines should bring the goal of self-sustained independence nearer.

A major difficulty at the present time, and one that cannot be eradicated immediately, is the deficiency in the output of university graduates and people with the appropriate level of intermediate education to meet the skilled manpower needs. Coupled with this is the growing problem of pupils completing primary school education seeking paid employment not immediately available for a considerable proportion of them. Another complication in the present situation, and one which is shared by other countries embarking upon similar efforts to grow socially, economically and politically, is the number of adults lacking the knowledge and the skills necessary for active participation in development projects. Whatever the long-term prospects of creating a well-designed and administered educational system to ensure the flow of skilled manpower into industry, commerce and administration, in many cases, the best immediate contribution to economic growth is to be obtained by giving adults the necessary instruction and training. But this requires at least a reasonable level of literacy. In 1948, in the Report on the Anchau Rural Development and Settlement Scheme, Dr. T. A. M. Nash remarked:

> Our work here would have been enormously simplified had there been one or two literates in every hamlet who could have read our messages to the hamlet heads. We must look forward to the day when every order from the Emir and District Head is nailed up on the village tree and the peasant really understands what he is supposed to do. . . . When the peasant can read the scales and work out how much he should get he will become a much wealthier man.*

In essence the educational issue is summed up in these three problems, how to provide in the shortest possible time men and women with the skills necessary to carry out the development programmes, how to assist the large numbers of young people

* T. A. M. Nash, *Report on the Anchau Rural Development and Settlement Scheme* (HMSO, London, 1948), p. 19.

with a modest modicum of education to fit them into the social and economic system in such a way as will give them hope and satisfaction, and how to educate the adult illiterate so that he may participate with understanding co-operation in a social and economic revolution that is not of his making.

Note. It will be noticed that there are differences in the population figures used in the main body of the text and the figures used in quoted passages. The figures used in the main body of the text are based upon the latest census. These figures have been subject to criticism on the grounds that they are inflated in favour of the Northern Region. Whatever inaccuracies may have occurred in the count, the figures are more likely to reflect the true population than any others and are undoubtedly a truer indication of the dimension of the population as a basis of planning than would be lower estimates.

CHAPTER 2

THE COUNTRY AND ITS PEOPLE

NIGERIA is a block of West Africa bordered on three sides by former French-governed countries and on the south by the Gulf of Guinea, which lies about 5 degrees north of the equator. After the First World War, a portion of the former German Cameroons was declared a mandated territory and Great Britain administered it as an integral part of Nigeria. After the Second World War the Cameroons was declared a United Nations trust territory, and as such continued to be administered by Great Britain. When Nigeria became independent, the Northern Cameroons territory agreed to integrate with Nigeria, the people of Southern Cameroons chose to join with the people of the former French-administered Cameroons to form a separate independent country.

In size, Nigeria is nearly four times the area of the United Kingdom, about equal in area to Pakistan and roughly equal to the combined area of Texas and Colorado. Within its 356,500 square miles live 55,653,821 people representing a mixture of various cultural and ethnic strains derived from successive migrations of Arab–Berber stock from the north-west and north-east and the indigenous Negro peoples of the more humid areas of the south. Nigeria is the most populous country of the African continent and the largest unit of people of African origin in the world. The average density of population is estimated at 158 persons to the square mile; but in some parts of the south-east, rural densities exceed 900 persons to the square mile. The distribution of the population density, however, is not always consistent with a favourable physical environment. In the south-western part of the Northern Region, the density of population sometimes falls below 25 persons to the square mile, and large sectors of the Middle Belt are virtually depopulated. Historical evidence suggests that in the past much of this region was under cultivation, but as a result of slave-raiding much of the land reverted to bush allowing the tsetse-fly to flourish. Furthermore, the slave-raiding led some communities to migrate to relatively inhospitable areas of land. In some parts of the Eastern Region overpopulation occurs in the dense rain forests with their poor heavily leached soils. One consequence of this maldistribution of population is that, whilst the country as a whole is self-sufficient in food production, some areas suffer from underproduction. Additionally, in consequence of the variations in population density, it is difficult to provide and develop the social services to the best advantage of the community as a whole.

The climate, vegetation and topography varies from the south to the north in a series of approximately parallel bands: a low coastal plain dominated by mangrove swamp has an annual mean temperature of 80°F, with comparatively small seasonal variations but with very high humidity. The rainfall ranges from less than 45 inches in its western section to more than 100 inches in the neighbourhood of Victoria in the east. Debundscha, on the western side of the Cameroon Mountain had 494 inches of rain in 1946. This belt of mangrove swamp varies in depth from 10 to 60 miles. It is followed by a zone 50–100 miles wide, of tropical rain forest and oil-palm bush. Rainfall varies from 40 inches annually in the west to 80 inches in the east. The mean annual temperature is between 75 and 80°F, with moderate seasonal variations. Northwards the tropical rain forest gives way to savannah as the general elevation of the land rises to 2000 feet. Annual rainfall decreases and in some places is less than 30 inches. Daily temperatures show much greater variation, and a long dry season from October to April is characterized by the harmattan dust-laden winds from the Sahara. Throughout the country dry and wet seasons are usually well marked, the dry season being shorter in the south than the north. The wet season is characterized by frequent and short rains, or squalls, increasing in frequency and duration nearer the coast.

The health and work pattern of the people is influenced less

directly by the climate than it is by dietary deficiences and the
high incidence and variety of diseases characteristic of underdeveloped tropical countries.

> Disease, malnutrition, and low agricultural productivity form, in fact, a
> vicious circle in Nigeria as in the remainder of Tropical Africa; the
> peasant, because of the multiplicity of diseases to which he is exposed and
> which sap his energy, is often an inefficient agriculturalist; because he is
> under-nourished he is more susceptible to the wide range of diseases to
> which he is exposed. The breaking of this vicious circle is one of the main
> problems facing the territory.*

Ranking with malnutrition as a major hazard to health in
Nigeria is malaria. Tuberculosis, smallpox, cerebrospinal
meningitis are other diseases of serious significance. Bilharzia,
guinea-worm and yaws contribute to the erroneously attributed
"indolence" of the people. Relatively few Nigerians are free of
worms of one kind or another in their intestines, and these,
together with bacillary and amoebic dysentery, contribute to
poor health. The high incidence of intestinal illness occurs during
the rainy season, the period of greatest agricultural activity. The
economic consequences of this are difficult to assess, but there is
undoubtedly a direct relationship between the incidence of
intestinal disease and productive efficiency. Leprosy, relapsing
fever and yellow fever are well on the way to being wiped out.
Sleeping-sickness and its companion disease in cattle has been
greatly reduced in significance, but still prevents the raising of
cattle over large areas of the country. The paucity of medical
facilities and the inevitably slow rate at which they can be provided are recognized as major handicaps to the country.

> The major emphasis of the Ministry of Health programme [in the Federal
> Government Development Plan 1962–8] will be on the training of doctors.
> The ratio of doctors to population in Nigeria is at present about 1 to 32,000.
> Clearly the present numbers of doctors is inadequate, particularly when it
> is realized that in many areas villages are situated as much as a hundred
> miles from the nearest medical facilities. Disease and injury take a severe
> toll of life and result in costly losses of labour, time, output and efficiency.
> The Government realizes therefore that a carefully co-ordinated health

* A. Brown, *Land and People of Nigeria*, K. M. Buchanan and J. C. Pugh
(University of London Press, London, 1955).

programme is essential, not only for the physical welfare of the Nation, but also to contribute to the increased productivity which is essential for the success of the Plan.*

Apart from the obvious educational implications in the provision of training facilities for doctors, nurses, medical auxiliaries and health workers, the situation calls for a major effort in health education in the schools and among the adult members of the community.

The extent to which this aspect of development has been realized by the Government of Nigeria is illustrated by the Akufo Village Scheme and the launching of the Ibarapa Project. Underlying the Akufo Village Scheme is the acceptance of the fact that

> irrespective of whether one is dealing with disease in urban or rural areas of Africa, the outstanding obstacles to a rational approach to disease control is the lack of valid statistical data relating to the African population, and describing its distribution, birth rates, death rates and incidence of disease in Africa can be soundly formulated, it will be necessary to receive substantial data on actual incidence of disease ... in both rural and urban areas.†

The Akufo Scheme, organized under the auspices of the University of Ibadan (Department of Medicine) with the collaboration of the Liverpool School of Tropical Medicine, is designed to study the village area in statistical and technical terms in order to focus attention on the community as a unit and to stress the importance in its health patterns of the interplay between diet, environment, social and genetic background in a rural population in Western Nigeria. One of the outcomes of the study emphasized the importance of orientating the curriculum of medical training in Nigeria in the direction of the current needs of the community if a rational approach to the development of a health service is to be attained.

The Ibarapa Project aims at providing facilities for (i) the teaching of the principles of community medicine to under-

* Federal Government of Nigeria, *National Development Plan, 1962–1968* (The Federal Ministry of Economic Development, Lagos, 1962).
† H. M. Gilles, *Akufo, An Environmental Study of a Nigerian Village Community* (University of Ibadan, Ibadan, 1964), p. 5.

graduate students, (ii) the determination of the form of health service most appropriate to such an area, (iii) the analysis of the medical needs of the community—both preventive and clinical, and (iv) the exploitation of the area as an epidemiological and research area.

Quite apart from the importance of these projects as pilot projects they highlight the fact that "in the last analysis improvement in the health of the rural population can only be achieved by a concerted co-operative effort between health worker, social worker, educator and agricultural engineer".*

Teachers of preventive medicine have to devise a curriculum aimed at attracting students to their field rather than to deter them from it. The approach hitherto "too frequently employed in the tropics which accentuates the dichotomy between preventive and curative medicine is not only out of place but doomed to failure".† In this respect the new preventive medicine curriculum being developed at Ibadan University, which is based on close integration of effort with the other relevant departments of the university and thus emphasizing the interrelationship of public health with the other disciplines, is a positive example of how the health problems of low-income countries in tropical areas generally might be attacked.

Agriculture, forestry and fishing provide the source of livelihood for something of the order of 80 per cent of the people and contribute approximately 61·75 per cent of the gross domestic product of the country. Services, transport and distribution, construction and civil engineering, and government make up approximately 31 per cent of the gross domestic product, and manufacturing and craft industries, minerals and a variety of other minor activities account for the remaining 7·5 per cent of the gross domestic product. The economic development of the country and the improvement of its living standards in the foreseeable future are therefore dependent upon growth and development of the agricultural sector more than upon anything else.

* *Ibid.*
† *Ibid.*, p. 52.

The arable land resources of the country are extensive and the water supply is abundant but ill distributed. The climate is so favourable to plant life that it is comparable with the best attainable anywhere in the world. Primitive production methods, land tenure and usufruct practices which inhibit industrialization of agriculture and mediocre soil fertility, however, result in comparatively low yields.

About 10 per cent of the total area of Nigeria is under cultivation for farm or tree crops, approximately 32 per cent is under forest, and the remaining 58 per cent is either left fallow or is uncultivated. Land tenure and usufruct systems are varied and complicated, but in essentials they are communal in character rights to land and usufruct being held by either a family group, a village group or a tribal group. Individual ownership is rare except in the former colony area in the neighbourhood of Lagos.

Of the field crops only groundnuts represent an export crop of any significance. Palm-oil products, which account for something like 30 per cent of the total exports in value, are cultivated and maintained almost entirely by individual farmers. Research and commercial plantations account for less than 1 per cent of the total output, but production per acre in plantations greatly exceeds production from individually owned groves.

Cocoa is second only to palm-oil produce in its contribution to Nigeria's export receipts and represents approximately one-seventh of world production.

Third in importance as an export crop are groundnuts, the only field crop of significance as an export product. But, in addition to its value as a source of edible oil, it is an important source of protein-rich food and as a nitrogen fixer in certain conditions is a soil-improving crop. Other export crops of importance include benniseed, cotton, rubber and bananas. A large number of minor crops, nuts and dried fruit, gums, spices, fibres, fresh fruits and juice products are exported in small quantities varying from year to year. The survey carried out by the mission of the International Bank for Reconstruction and Development, whilst indicating clearly the potential for growth

of the agricultural sector of the country's economy, also emphasized the need for research into production and processing,
marketing, soils and the control of diseases. Similar problems
have to be faced in the development of the domestic crops and
livestock. In the case of the latter, the maximum export potential
for hides and skins products cannot be realized until the heavy
incidence of skin diseases is remedied and the traditional processing techniques are improved.

In 1954 it was estimated that a fourfold increase in the livestock production was justified on account of the deficiency of
the Nigerian diet in animal protein and milk alone. The improvement of breeds of stock and the improved control of diseases
affecting stock generally is essential. But such improvements
will not provide the increases required until the scourge of the
tsetse-fly is removed and large areas of the country are reclaimed
for stock-raising. The possibilities of doing this have been demonstrated by Dr. T. A. M. Nash. Related to the improvement of
the stock and the control of disease is the need for soil and pasture
improvement. Effective measures in these respects would provide
the means of dealing with the problem of the nomadic Fulani,
the most skilful graziers and breeders of livestock in the country.
The World Bank Mission reporting on this aspect of the country's
economy commented:

> Fulani cattle have a strong constitution, are admirably suited to their
> environment and living conditions and are among the finest to be found
> in Africa. Their various breeds provide excellent foundation stock for
> both beef and milk production; great care should be taken to avoid
> degeneration through too drastic change in the Fulani husbandry prac-
> tices.
>
> Stabilization of the Fulani is considered of major importance in the
> expansion of livestock production. There are indications that many Fulani
> would prefer to follow a settled existence. Nomadism has probably been a
> matter of necessity rather than of choice; if permanent water and year-
> round tsetse-free pastures can be developed, the need for seasonal move-
> ment will disappear, although the excellent practice of rotational grazing
> should continue.*

* International Bank for Reconstruction and Development, *The Economic
Development of Nigeria* (Johns Hopkins Press, Baltimore, 1955), p. 263.

A complication in the situation is that the Fulani have few, if any land rights in Nigeria. At present they are tolerated because they do not damage standing crops; but the expansion of cultivation and the development of mixed farming will exclude them from many of their traditional grazing grounds.

Fish have traditionally been an important item of the Nigerian diet, but river and lagoon fishing has been carried out with little appreciation of the balance of the life cycle. Itinerant fishing to obtain the maximum catch in as short a time as possible and often by highly destructive means is common. With an increasing population and larger markets available for immediate sale of the catches there is danger that the fish population of the rivers may be seriously depleted. The great variations in width and depth of streams between the rainy and the dry seasons result in heavy losses of fish; they get stranded in pools which dry up after the floods subside. It might be possible to prevent this by river control, but the presence in highly aerated waters of the carrier of onchoceriasis (river blindness) makes it a complex operation.

Sea fishing is still a relatively small contributor to the supply of fish-food except for bonga and shrimp fishing near the estuaries of the big rivers. In fish production as in crop production the situation is one with considerable potential for growth and there is great need for the organization of the trade and for research.

The forests of Nigeria have for centuries provided a large proportion of the people with shelter, food and fuel, with spices, drugs, fibres, gums, resins, tanning material, dyes, oil seeds and nuts. In addition, the forests have been a source of export timber varying in recent years from 10 to 13 million cubic feet a year in addition to domestic consumption of the order of 15 million cubic feet a year.

Today, 32 per cent of the area of Nigeria is classified as forest land. Seven-eighths of the area, however, is of value for firewood only, and of the high forest only some 2000 square miles have economic value in terms of commercial timber. In the past it was assumed that under the favourable environmental conditions regeneration would occur naturally and that the main problem of exploitation was merely that of extraction. It is now recognized that this is not so, and that a national programme for maintaining and replenishing forests is essential if a sound basis for permanent exploitation is to be established. If this is provided the forestry resources offer considerable prospects of substantially increased returns to the economy as a whole. The more efficient exploitation of the forests both for the expansion of timber exports and an increase in domestic consumption of timber and firewood will, however, require understanding and co-operation from the people. Except in the Western Region, management of forest reserves has, up to the present, not been possible.

Nigeria is not lacking in the ingredients needed for industrial development. Mineral resources include tin, columbite, lead, zinc, gold, iron, ceramic clays, quartz, feldspar, silica, sand, limestone, coal and oil. Water is available in inexhaustible supplies, and, whilst power-generating capacity is low, there is sufficient potential available to absorb a moderate expansion of the industrial load. With a population of 55 million still expanding there is a home market of great importance and a good labour supply. What is lacking is investment capital and skilled human experience.

Commenting upon the labour situation in 1954, the World Bank Mission remarked:

> The general agricultural underemployment provides a reservoir of potential industrial labor, and a preference for cash income causes many persons to migrate to the towns. Labor moves freely even from region to region, despite differences in religion and custom. This is particularly true of the Eastern Ibo and the Northern Hausa, the one because of competitive conditions at home and the other motivated at least in part by trading traditions.
>
> Differences in productivity seem to depend less on inherent attributes of the workers than upon the quality of the management and training supplied. For example, the mission could not fail to be impressed with the rapid advance and high output of labor in the Ibadan cigarette factory and the Sapele plywood mill, or the success of the training programs of Shell-d'Arcy at Owerri—all three outstanding but by no means isolated illustrations.*

* *Ibid.*, p. 348.

Up to the present time, the comparative absence of local industry has given little opportunity for Nigerians to develop managerial skills and little incentive to seek technical qualifications. Furthermore, for generations the Nigerian has associated social status, the exercise of responsibility, security and the means of enjoying Western material standards of comfort with government employment. The combination of these factors still tend to inhibit the flow of persons with the requisite standards of general education into industry and commerce and into private business.

The people belong to some 250 different tribes. The former British administration defined the term tribe as "one or more clans descended from one legendary ancestor, though the legend may have been lost; originally observing one common shrine, though the memory may have been lost; speaking one language, though perhaps not the same dialect, and enlarged by assimilated peoples". The tribal units vary in membership from millions to a few thousand. Each region is dominated by a major tribe. In the Northern Region the Hausa people are dominant, with the Fulani, Kanuri, Tiv and Nupe forming significant minority elements. In the Western Region the Yoruba are the dominant people, in the Mid-Western Region the Edo people are the major tribe, and in the Eastern Region the Ibo people form the overwhelming majority. The tribal divisions are accompanied by cultural differences and linguistic differences that have a bearing upon the attitudes and relationships between the different regions.

In the north, Mohammedanism is the dominant religion, and its concepts are the basis of the family and the general social structure. Within the Islamic society the emirs still exercise feudal rights of overlordship. Pockets of older indigenous groups of inhabitants have survived still practising the animistic religions and organizing their lives upon clan patterns of society. In the Western Region the religious affiliations of the people are divided approximately equally between Islam, Christianity and indigenous animistic faiths. Islam appears to be growing in strength and differs from practice in the north, in that modern liberal sects have a significant following. In the Mid-West and Eastern Regions Islam has gained little support, Christianity and animistic faiths being almost equally supported. The religious differences have not given rise to serious clashes between adherents, but there have at times been minor clashes between sects in the southern areas of the country, and the Catholic and Protestant differences have cut across the provision of education.

The differences between the different languages are such that the evolution of a single Nigerian language as the national language was and is not possible. Neither is any one local language so widely used that it could become the lingua franca for the whole country, though Hausa has been considered by a few interested persons, as possibly capable of being so used. It is the lingua franca of the north. In the schools the early stages of instruction are carried out in the major language of the district. English becomes the language of instruction in the upper levels of the school system at different stages in the different regions. It is also the language of government, administration, commerce and industry, with the caveat, that at local levels of activity the indigenous language may be used. In this respect the English language probably serves as a unifying agency in the country as a whole.

This is a matter of some importance. Because each region is dominated by one tribal group and because there are other differentiating features (such as the traditional organizations of government), in the main groups have developed a strong regional pride that has grown stronger in some respects as a result of the regional political autonomy provided within the constitution of the Federation.

Politically the country is divided into four autonomous regions: Northern, Eastern, Western and the Mid-West. There is also a small federal territory which includes the Federal capital, Lagos. As has already been pointed out, each region has a predominant tribal group and other distinguishing social characteristics.

The Northern Region is the largest geographical unit (281,782 square miles) and also has the largest population 29,777,986.

Its predominant tribal group is the Hausa–Fulani in which the Hausa element is numerically predominant but the Fulani are the dominant ruling element. This reflects the fact that the Hausa people were the first invaders from the north in recent times to subordinate the local indigenous people, and they in turn were subordinated by the later Fulani invaders. The Fulani people consist of two groups—those who settled in the towns and became known as the town Fulani and those who continued their semi-nomadic, pastoral mode of life and are referred to as the cow Fulani. The town Fulani provide the ruling emirate families and are politically the more significant. Unlike the cow Fulani who have little to do with other peoples, the town Fulani have, to a considerable extent, intermarried with the Hausa. As a result of Lord Lugard's policy of indirect rule through the emirs and limited permission for Christian missionaries to work in Northern Nigeria, the region has remained predominantly Moslem, and political power has remained, very largely, with the emirs. The social system is still to a great extent a feudal one, and political control is exercised by Alhaji Sir Ahmadu Bello, leader of the Northern People's Congress, who is generally regarded as the most powerful man in Nigeria.

The Western Region, the second largest of the regions (30,454 square miles and a population of 10,278,500) is populated mainly by the Yoruba, who, whilst keeping a hierarchical form of chieftainship with certain electoral features, has developed a vigorous regional parliamentary system of government. Until 1963 the Action Group led by Chief Obafemi Awolowo dominated the political scene in the region, but a split in the party resulted in a brief interregnum when the administration was put in charge of a federal administrator. The regional government now consists of a splinter group from the Action Party, the United Peoples Party and the National Convention of Nigerian Citizens. The latter is the dominant party of the Eastern Region and was founded by the present Governor-General, Nnamdi Azikiwe. The Yoruba people are the most urbanized of the Nigerian peoples; about 30 per cent of them live in towns of 20,000 people or more, with Ibadan, the regional capital having a population of more than a million. By contrast the urban element of the population of the Northern Region is only 4 per cent and the urban element of the Eastern Region is about 7 per cent of the regional populations respectively.

The Eastern Region is the most densely inhabited part of the country with 12,388,646 people occupying an area of 29,484 square miles. Traditionally the political organization of the people followed the pattern of the extended family rather than tribal pattern with leadership vested in hierarchical or semi-hierarchical chiefs. The status of the chief, unlike that of the chiefs in the west or the emirs in the north being largely honorific and without political authority.

The newly-formed Mid-West Region, consisting of the Benin and Delta provinces, previously were part of the Western Region. It is 14,922 square miles in area and has a population of 2,533,337.

At the Federal level there is a coalition government of the National Convention of Nigerian Citizens Party and the Northern Peoples Congress Party. The latter have an absolute majority in Parliament, and the Prime Minister, Alhaji Sir Abubakar Tafawa Balewa, is a member of the Party. The Action Group, under the leadership of Chief Obafemi Awolowo, provided an active parliamentary Opposition until just over two years ago Awolowo was arrested for treason, found guilty and imprisoned. Since then the Opposition has had no clear leading spokesman.

There is considerable tension between the parties at the Federal level, and the failure of any party to gain effective power outside their home regions has increased regional pride, a tendency to seek extension of regional autonomy. Despite these centrifugal forces, there is throughout the country a strong sense of Nigerian national consciousness.

The Federal Government has exclusive responsibility for foreign affairs, the monetary system, national defence, the railways, the major ports, the major highways and the communications system, and through statutory corporations has a virtual monopoly of a number of other enterprises. Approximately two-thirds of the revenue of the regional governments is provided by the Federal Government.

The tendency to regionalization is closely related to the tribal and social pattern of the Nigerian society, but also, in part, reflects something of the history of the British presence in Nigeria.

Prior to Islamic and Western contact with the peoples of this part of Africa, little is known of the history of the region. Myth, legend and oral tradition indicate the existence of tribal groups of varying size with political organizations of varying complexity and relatively great stability. Archaeological finds indicate the existence of highly sophisticated art forms among many of the separate communities. For the most part the different groups were self-contained and had little intercourse of any kind with their neighbours. Traditions point to migratory movements at intervals penetrating the area from the north-east and the north-west. There appears to have been comparatively little population movement along the coast, and what there was appears to have been largely movement from the western area of the Niger delta to the founding of settlements at what we now know as Lagos and Accra.

With the establishment of Islamic rule in the north and European trade in the south at a number of points on the coast, historical data increased in quantity. British influence became significant in the country as a whole just over a hundred years ago, and British administration was established in 1903 when the submission of Sokoto and Kano was followed by the emirates of Katsena and Gando accepting British supremacy. The conditions of settlement imposed, included the passing of all rights of conquest from the Fulani to Great Britain; sultans, emirs and principal officers of state holding appointments from the British Government in obedience to the laws of the British Government, and that they should no longer buy and sell slaves, nor enslave people, and that they should import no firearms except flint-locks, that they should enforce no sentences in their courts of law which were repugnant to British practice, and that the British Government should in future hold rights in land and taxation.

In the south British presence was a matter of slave-trading and exploration until 1861 when possession was taken of Lagos with the object of checking the slave-trade in that region. As late as 1865, a parliamentary committee recommended a policy which would, if followed, have led to the ultimate withdrawal of official British influence from the coast, and the consulate at Lokoja was abandoned.

In 1879 private British trading interests, in the face of the challenge of two French firms supported by the French Government, amalgamated to form the United Africa Company. In 1884 the latter bought out the French interests. In 1886 the United Africa Company received a royal charter and became the Royal Niger Company. As a result of the Berlin Conference, the coast lands known as the Oil Rivers became a British protectorate under the control of the Royal Niger Company. Between that date and 1909, Anglo-French interests were in conflict in the west of the territory. The situation was such that in 1900 the company surrendered its charter and the territories were designated by the name Nigeria and were placed under the political control of the Crown. Boundary demarcations were agreed with the French in the west and north and with the Germans in the east.

The various parts of the country were amalgamated in 1904, but provincial organization continued to follow the tripartite division of the country. The adoption of a policy of indirect rule through the traditional instruments of chiefs also served to emphasize the differences between the south-east, the south-west and the north.

In economic terms British rule, until 1929, meant development as a result of normal colonial enterprise and commerce under private stimulus. By 1911 a railway had been built from Lagos to Kano. In 1920 Lord Lugard, the Governor-General, produced the first attempt at a development programme. Apart from an element of Empire preference no attempt was made to provide Nigeria with a sheltered market for its exports, and as a producer of primary products of a limited range the country felt the full impact of the world slumps in the twenties and the thirties. Despite assistance under the Colonial Development and Welfare Acts of 1929 and 1940 the economy of the country made no significant progress. Under the 1945 Act much more generous provision was made. At the same time the Nigerian Government took steps to provide an overall development plan.

It is difficult to assess exactly to what extent this movement towards planned development accelerated economic growth. But there was a substantial amount of growth, for whereas the gross domestic product of 1950 was about £700 million in 1960 it had risen to about £1023 million. This represents a growth rate of about 4 per cent per annum. During the same period the amount of gross fixed investment, roads, schools, housing, plant and other fixed capital assets rose from about £1 million to about £106,900,000, representing an increase from about 7 per cent of the gross domestic product to about 15 per cent. As the gross consumer expenditures also rose during the period from £609,400,000 to £870 million and that the rise was greater than the population increase, there was also an improvement in the general standard of living. During the same period the expenditure on education rose from £3,100,000 to £26,300,000.

This rate of economic growth compares favourably with that of most other underdeveloped countries during this period. But it could have been considerably better were it not for a number of serious militating factors. Although some improvement in the literacy rate on the 12 per cent registered in the 1952–3 census has been made the educational attainment of the country as a whole still falls far short of the requirements necessary for industrial development. Not only is the greater part of the labour force still engaged in agricultural pursuits but nearly 60 per cent of the force is still engaged in subsistence farming rather than for the market. A study of the sources of consumer and capital goods and of raw materials for processing carried out by Mr. Ojetunde Aboyade of Ibadan University in 1959 revealed that 48 per cent of soft consumer goods, 10 per cent of durable consumer goods, 30 per cent of capital goods and 11 per cent of the processing and raw materials were imported. Whilst the rate of domestic savings has been maintained at about 10 per cent of the gross domestic product, which is a high rate for an underdeveloped country, a substantial export surplus in 1954 changed into an import surplus with a consequential drop in the sterling assets of the country. In part, this weakness reflects the dependence of the country upon the movements of world prices for primary products which have been falling, and, in part, it is due to effect of adverse weather conditions on the agricultural output. In part the slowing down of the rate of growth of the gross domestic product also reflects the extent to which investments have been concentrated upon the development of the social services of housing, health and education and upon projects that are slow to produce results.

CHAPTER 3

DEVELOPMENT OF MODERN EDUCATION, 1571–1925

THE Portuguese merchant adventurers gave the people of what we now know as Nigeria their first experience of education as practised in Europe. From the beginning of their trading enterprises overseas in the fifteenth century, education was regarded by the Portuguese as of fundamental importance to the spread of Christianity. This opinion was held by ecclesiastical and civil authorities alike. In 1515 missionaries who visited Benin obtained the permission of the Oba of Benin to teach his son and the sons of a number of other chiefs the rudiments of the Christian faith. A mission which reached Benin in 1539 found a Christian Negro, who was held prisoner by the Oba, teaching boys to read.

In 1571 on the island of São Thome, off the coast of Nigeria, a seminary was established to train young men for the priesthood. There is evidence that missionaries from São Thome visited Warri, the chief town of the Itsekiri tribe during the sixteenth and seventeenth centuries, and the number of people taught to read was enough to create some demand for Portuguese books.

These and similar attempts to introduce Western education into Nigeria were limited to a few scattered trading centres. With the growth of the transatlantic slave-trade in the sixteenth and seventeenth centuries, the legitimate trading centres declined and made no educational impact upon the people living in the interior of the country.

It was not until the last quarter of the eighteenth century that Western education made any significant impact upon Nigeria. The resurgence of Christian and humanitarian concern for the brotherhood of man and the dignity of the individual resulted, among other things, in the movement for the abolition of slavery. At the same time, the evangelical movement which gave new energy and life to the Christian Church in Europe also stimulated a concern for the emancipation and regeneration of peoples in other lands. Out of this concern for the spiritual well-being of the people of Africa and Asia grew the missionary movement. In Britain, the Baptist Missionary Society was founded in 1792, the London Missionary Society in 1795, and in 1799 the Church Missionary Society.

This efflorescence of missionary endeavour coincided with European interest in the commercial and political drive to penetrate the interior of the continent. Whilst the missionary effort was concerned with the redemption and the regeneration of the people of the "Dark Continent" it was also concerned with the material well-being of the people. The Bible and the plough were seen to be complementary. In consequence, missionaries, traders, explorers and, later, government agents collaborated in opening up the continent.

The first missionary contact in modern times in Nigeria was made on 24 September 1842 when the Rev. Thomas Freeman and Mr. and Mrs. de Graft of the Wesleyan Methodist Mission in the Gold Coast arrived at Badagry, started a mission there and built a school. Thomas Freeman also travelled inland to Abeokuta to visit immigrants including refugees from the slave-raiders. There he started a second mission station also with a small school.

The next group of missionaries to arrive in the country, some months later, were Samuel Crowther, a Yoruba who had been rescued by a British naval vessel from a slave-trading ship, a Mr. Townsend and the Rev. C. A. Golmer. All three were members of the Church Missionary Society. They landed at Badagry from Sierra Leone, and in 1846 they reached Abeokuta; there they built a mission, a church and a school. By 1849 the CMS Yoruba Mission had established four main stations at Badagry, Lagos, Abeokuta and Ibadan. There were five native ordained missionaries, and forty-two trained native teachers working in sixteen schools with a total enrolment of 895 pupils. In 1959 the mission opened a grammar school at Lagos, beginning with six pupils for whom school fees were charged. At Abeokuta a training institution, known as the Theological Seminary, provided instruction in English, mathematics and New Testament Greek for men intended to serve in the ministry of the Church. In addition, training was also given in printing and carpentry. In the schools instruction was given in Yoruba and in English. The Bible, the Prayer Book, a Hymn Book and school textbooks were all printed in Yoruba.

Anna Hinderer, the wife of the first CMS missionary to open up work at Ibadan, has provided a record of the school work and the Sunday school work in the journal which she kept. The content of the teaching, and the attitude taken towards it, is clearly expressed in this entry in her *Memorials*, published in 1873:

> I have had a treat to-day, my sixteen school-children to dinner. It was a real pleasure to me to see them getting on so nicely, four of them now begin to read the Yoruba Testament; all have learned Watt's little catechism, which has been translated, and the commandments; two are also learning the English primer; they extremely like to learn English sentences . . . I am teaching them to sew and knit for I want an occupation for them as the school only lasts from nine to twelve.*

Miss Tucker, who was stationed at Abeokuta, writing in 1853, describes how Mr. Crowther established a school in Abeokuta and that Mrs. Crowther taught the boys to sew, "for in Yoruba the men alone are considered worthy of being initiated into the mysteries of needlework".

Important as was the establishment of schools and training institutions, in some ways the Sunday schools for adults were more important. A description of a school, also recorded by Mrs. Hinderer, provides a clear picture of the organization and the content of the instruction.

> The first bell rings at half-past eight: from then till a few minutes before nine, when the second bell rings, we can look out and see our people coming, with their nice English bags of coloured print, or their own grass bags, on their heads, containing their books; some with only the Primer,

* A. Hinderer, *Seventeen Years in the Yoruba Country* (Seeley, Jackson & Halliday, London, 1873), p. 81.

others more advanced in the new art of reading, with various portions of the Word of God; St. Luke, the Psalms, Proverbs, and Genesis, being among the great favourites. Now the whole of the New Testament is complete, and bound in one volume, and our people will, I know, be much delighted with such a volume. We see our people hastening towards us as nine o'clock approaches, for the one hour of school is too precious to be wasted by being five minutes too late. The school consists of men and women, who are most anxiously and diligently reading, and learning to read; men on one side of the church, and women on the other. We have to use our more advanced day-scholars as teachers for some classes, and it is very pretty to see the thankfulness and attention of these men and women, some with grey hairs, to their young teachers, and they often bring them presents of honey or fruit, to tempt these children to go on teaching them when the school is over. We have about eight or nine classes of different stages; and a very interesting assembly, at the bottom of the church, of those who cannot learn to read. We gather these together, and first tell them a short simple Bible story, and let them tell it us again, to see that they remember it, and take it in. Then we teach them a text, or a verse of a hymn, and the last quarter of an hour is always given in all the classes to teaching by repetition some catechism, and sometimes for a change we have the whole school together to go over the Creed, the Lord's Prayer, and the Ten Commandments, to make sure they are not forgotten.*

The picture presented was repeated with minor variations in content and method at all the mission stations. Whilst the educational effort was primarily directed to making the converts "People of the Book", it also provided the initial education of the men who later were to become schoolmasters for the schools, priests for the churches and clerical assistants for commerce and government. The bookishness of the instruction provided has been the subject of critical remarks by many commentators of missionary educational effort. Too frequently, however, the critics have failed to note that the bookishness was the direct consequence of the educational purpose pursued by the missionaries, and that the demand from commerce and government for educated persons also placed a premium on book learning rather than on practical skills.

The initial missionary effort in Western Nigeria was soon followed by enterprises in the Niger delta and Eastern Nigeria. Under the leadership of Bishop Crowther and with the co-

* *Ibid.*, p. 296.

operation of the Niger explorer, M'Gregor Laird, the CMS Niger Mission was established at Bonny in 1863, having been preceded by a visit to Onitsha in 1857. In 1847 the United Free Church of Scotland started work at Calabar. In 1853 the American Southern Baptist Convention began work at Oyo, founded the Baptist Academy at Lagos, and developed a vocational and trades school at Abeokuta. The Roman Catholic Mission established schools in Lagos when they began work there in 1868, and in 1872 four Sisters from France organized education for girls. The Roman Catholic work was at first directed mainly to people repatriated from Brazil, and until 1876 the instruction was carried out in Portuguese. In the same year an Irish Father opened the school that is now known as St. Gregory's, and teaching in English was introduced. In 1882 teaching in English was made compulsory.

For nearly half a century the entire educational provision was dependent upon the efforts of the Christian missions supported by their home churches and gifts from friends. Until 1877, apart from passing an Ordinance in 1822, to govern education in all the West African territories and a visit in 1864–5 by Commissioner Ord to examine the state of education in the territories, neither the local nor the Imperial government made any provision for education in Nigeria. In 1877 the Lagos administration made grants of £200 to each of the three missionary societies carrying out educational work in the Colony. Apart from this financial contribution, the administration had nothing to do with education in any way. The grants were made annually until 1882 when the West African Education Ordinance was applied to the Colony of Lagos. Under the Ordinance a Board of Education was established, consisting of the Governor, the members of the Executive Council, and four nominated members. The general Board had power to set up local boards to advise the general Board on "conditions under which grants were made to schools" and whether the conditions were being fulfilled; and on the opening of government schools. The Ordinance led to a system of grants-in-aid awarded for good organization and discipline together with special grants based in part on the numbers of pupils enrolled, and, in part, on the results of examinations. In addition the Ordinance required that the Settlement of Lagos should contribute one-third of the salary of Her Majesty's Inspector of Schools for the West African Colonies.

In 1886 Lagos and the part of the interior country under its control was made an independent colony and protectorate, separate from the Gold Coast Colony, and the first purely Nigerian Education Ordinance was enacted. Among other things the Ordinance provided for members of the Legislative Council to replace members of the Executive Council on the Board of Education, defined more specifically the conditions under which grants were to be made to schools, and provided scholarships of £10 per annum for poor children to attend secondary schools. Despite these provisions, education continued to be virtually the monopoly of the Christian missions. The first non-mission school was not founded until 1901, when the Government established a school for Moslem children in Lagos. In 1902 Mr. Henry Carr, a Yoruba and one of the first graduates of Fourah Bay College, Sierra Leone, in his Report as Inspector of Schools commented upon the unsatisfactory provisions and remarked that "a really suitable system of education cannot be cheap and cannot be provided under the voluntary system". Yet, in 1960, when Nigeria became independent the mission educational agencies were still responsible for over 70 per cent of the schools in the Western and Eastern Regions and the federal territory of Lagos.

In Northern Nigeria missionary education activity developed much more slowly and on a smaller scale. This was in part, due to the agreement made between the British Government and the emirs following the pacification of the north, when it was agreed that Christian missionaries should not be admitted to the emirates without the consent of the emirs. This resulted in missionary effort being largely confined to the pagan areas. Apart from the administrative restrictions upon mission educational effort, there was antagonism towards Western education due to the existence of a loose system of Qur'anic schools. In these schools boys, and occasionally girls, learnt by heart large sections of the Qur'an, were trained in correct methods of worship and taught the basic laws of social conduct by the local *mallam* or teacher. Instruction lasted for from eight to twelve years or more, and, for those who wished, opportunity for advanced instruction was available from an Alkali or Imam with a special reputation for his learning. Apart from the risk that a European type of schooling might make the pupils indifferent to the faith, there was a general antipathy towards things Western. The existence of a large number of the Qur'anic schools (in 1913 one estimate stated that the number of schools was 19,073 with an attendance of 143,312) and the degree of attachment that the majority of the population showed to this traditional form of education, made the introduction of Western education very difficult. The Government, however, decided at an early date to make some provision for Western education for the north.

In 1909, as a result of studies of educational practices in Egypt, the Anglo-Egyptian Sudan, the Gold Coast and Lagos, carried out by an administrative officer, the policy for education in the north was based upon the provision of schools through the agency of the Native Administrations. Hausa, the local lingua franca and language of the dominant group, was made the medium of instruction in the elementary schools. A few advanced central schools were established in which English was taught. Religion and the Arabic language received a prominent place in the curriculum and the traditional conformities of the Moslem society in dress, salutations, courtesies and the accepted code of the local society constituted the major part of instruction given. The education of girls received no attention until 1928 when a Lady Superintendent of education was posted to Ilorin. Between 1930 and 1936 schools for girls were opened at Kano, Katsina, Sokoto, Birnin Kebbi and Argungu. In that year there were 600 girls attending school in the north. The main items of their instruction were domestic subjects and hygiene.

In the country generally, Western education was identified with evangelization. Professor Victor Murray in his book, *The*

School in the Bush, commented: "To all intents and purposes the school is the Church. Right away in the bush or in the forest the two are one, and the village teacher is also the village evangelist. An appreciation of this fact is cardinal in all considerations of African education."*

Whilst this identification inhibited the development of education in Northern Nigeria, in the rest of the country it contributed to the growth of a new social group which provided the leadership for the new nationalism of the twentieth century.

The approach to education pursued by the missionaries was based upon the certainty of the Christian message, but it was also based upon the assumption of the superiority of Western civilization and the evil character of paganism. African customs, beliefs and practices, family life and even the institution of chiefdom were, with few exceptions, regarded as repugnant. Christianity was confused with Western civilization. The Nigerian was to be remade in the image that the missionaries brought with them. The critics of the missionary effort found it easy to comment adversely upon the way in which missionary education produced people who became political agitators, possessing no roots in nor respect for local traditions, beliefs or environment, out of touch with the mass of the people, ridiculously sensitive to racial and social discrimination, real or fancied, ready to create and respond to unrest.

These strictures had an element of truth in them, but despite the deficiencies of the education which was provided, from it did emerge an excellent body of men without whose services neither Church, nor State, nor trade would have made progress.

The criticism of missionary education in Africa generally was summed up in 1922 by Dr. Thomas Jesse Jones in the Report of the Phelps–Stokes Commission, *Education in Africa*:

> Though educational facilities in Africa are largely credited to missions and a really great service has been rendered by them to the Native people, many of the missions have yet to realize the full significance of education in the development of the African people. The defects in the educational

* A. V. Murray, *The School in the Bush* (Longmans, London, 1929).

program, so far as they exist, have usually been due to their conception of education. Some have thought of education merely as the imparting of information, or, at most, as the development of the mind without relation to the moral and spiritual life. To such a group education has no religious significance. Others have thought of education as necessary chiefly to enable the Natives to read the Bible and to understand the spirit of Christianity. This group has been content with education in books. For the masses they have provided the three R's. For the catechists and the advanced pupils they have endeavoured to give a knowledge of literature, including, of course, an interpretation of religion. In this limiting education to class-room instruction in books, missionaries were following the ideals prevailing in their home country . . . the missions have failed to see how their success depends on native welfare, and have therefore been strangely indifferent to the economic value of agriculture, and little concerned with the health and morals of the people.*

These remarks were made on behalf of a group of people, some of whom were missionaries themselves, and all of whom accorded unstinted admiration to the devotion and self-sacrifice of missionaries. The obvious defects, however, are but a part of the story. For not only were the missionaries themselves aware of the inadequacies, but they also tried to devise a system of education suited to the country's needs. At Abeokuta, Lagos, Onitsha and Calabar different missions had established industrial and vocational training, including in the instruction teaching about the cleaning and packing of agricultural produce for the European markets, brick and tile making, carpentry, masonry, tailoring, printing, and so on. A good deal of missionary effort was directed to what was known in government and commercial circles as the Basle method. This was a system of making mission stations self-supporting by cultivating farms, training and employing carpenters and masons, and having a trade section to dispose of their surplus produce. Until the close of the nineteenth century, frequent reference was made by government administrators, commercial agents and local leaders of public opinion in Lagos to the merits of combining liberal education and training for trade and industry. The reason why the missions did not do more of this kind of work was that it cost more. Seminaries,

* L. J. Lewis (ed.), *Phelps–Stokes Reports on Education in Africa* (edited and abridged, Oxford University Press, London, 1962), p. 9.

teacher-training colleges and secondary grammar schools were much cheaper to provide and organize and were far cheaper to run than were industrial schools. Furthermore, economic expansion was still largely confined to commerce based upon the export of the primary products. In fact, there was little call for industrial training, and the development of industry had to wait upon commercial expansion. For the latter, clerical training was the immediate priority. Even in 1899, when the Government established the first government secondary school in Lagos, they chose to make it a grammar type of school, and this despite a record of thirty years of criticism of the provision of too bookish a schooling by the missions. The country still needed more clerks than the school system was capable of producing.

One other consideration must also be kept in mind when assessing the worth of the mission educational effort after this period. The Africans themselves knew what they wanted of the schools. In Bonny, the chiefs, who found the money for the schools, told the missionaries that "they did not want religious teaching, of that the children have enough at home; they teach them that themselves; that they want them to be taught how to gauge palm oil and other such mercantile business as soon as possible". Western education was relevant in respect of those things in which the European excelled, and the obvious excellence lay in their business methods. Within the pattern of African family life the child learned the moral and religious concepts of his own society, that learning being reinforced by long-established taboos. His intellect was trained through the conundrums, fables, games, alliterative verse and the telling of the tribal lays. The Western school, on the other hand, was the source of other kinds of knowledge and skills; reading and writing, science, those techniques which gave the white man so much power. It was Western schooling that equipped the African, Ferguson, to become the Governor of Lagos, that enabled the ex-slave boy Samuel Adjayi Crowther to become the first Nigerian Bishop of the Anglican Church, Henry Carr to become Inspector of Schools in 1892.

From the missionary schools came that section of African society that was in close contact with the Western world, the kinds of people most needed at the time. These were clerks, teachers and agents who did those tasks which made the growth of a peasant economy possible. Without such provision, neither administration nor commerce could have been serviced adequately.

In 1912 an Imperial Conference was held in London to review the provision of education in the Colonial Empire.* The primary educational facilities then available in southern Nigeria and the Colony of Lagos, consisted of fifty-five government and native administration schools with a total enrolment of 3984 pupils; ninety-one mission schools in receipt of government grants with an enrolment of 11,732 pupils; in addition there were approximately 20,000 pupils in mission primary schools which received no assistance from government funds. At the secondary level, there were four mission schools receiving government assistance; five schools which were unassisted, and one government school. Of three mission training colleges for teachers only one was in receipt of grants; government made no provision itself for training teachers for the government and native administration schools.

The outbreak of the First World War in 1914 put an end to any prospect of expanding the provision of education. Government responsibility for education was, however, given clear recognition, and the Governor-General, Lord Lugard, in a Memorandum on Education in 1919 declared:

> I regard it as an essential feature of a right policy in Education that it should enlist in hearty co-operation all educational agencies in the country which are conducted (as Mission schools are) with the sole object of benefiting the people. . . . Unassisted Schools are independent of Government control, but I hope that they will be induced to conform to the principles and policy laid down by Government, and supported and approved by the principal educational agencies.

* Imperial Education Conference Papers III—*Education System of the Chief Colonies not possessing Responsible Government. Southern Nigeria* (HMSO, London, 1913).

To encourage the transfer of unassisted schools to the assisted list, Lord Lugard suggested in 1912 that the "payment by results" system of awarding grants made as a result of an annual examination of the pupils in selected subjects should be replaced by a system of frequent inspections and examining throughout the school year. The general tone of the school, discipline, organization and moral instruction could earn a school up to 30 per cent of the assessment mark; up to 20 per cent could be awarded for the efficiency and adequacy of the staff; periodical examinations and general progress could earn up to 40 per cent; buildings, equipment and sanitation represented the remaining portion of the assessment, namely 10 per cent.

Whatever disagreement there might be with this system of evaluating the worth of a school for grant-earning purposes, it produced a marked increase in the number of schools included in the assisted list. Even so, a considerable number of schools remained outside the aided system. Some of these were regarded as very unsatisfactory. Lord Lugard believed them to be a handicap to educational development, and of some of the private-venture schools he suggested that: "Many or most of them are stated to be conducted for profit by half-educated youths and others, who are quite incompetent to teach, and over whom local chiefs find it very difficult to exercise control."

Attempts were made to control these schools by means of compulsory inspection and application of power held by the Governor to close unsatisfactory schools, but with little success. By 1926 the number of unassisted schools had grown to 3578 with a nominal enrolment of 146,700 children and an average attendance of 96,600.

Lord Lugard's successor, Sir Hugh Clifford, saw this development as inimical to both educational and social progress. In an attempt to deal more effectively with it, he vested his powers of closure in the Board of Education, and advocated that the management of all elementary education in the Southern Province should be placed in the hands of the missions. This was a reversal of government policy which had previously been directed towards increasing government participation with the co-operation of local communities.

Despite the efforts made by Lord Lugard and his successor, the latter summing up the general characteristics of education in Africa in 1925 had this to say:

> The Local Government and the various mission societies in each dependency share between them the task of education. In some of the dependencies the missions have borne the entire burden; in all, they have hitherto had the preponderant share. The governments, at first absorbed in building up the administrative machinery and introducing law and order, and latterly engrossed in the difficulties caused by the war, and its immediate aftermath, are now for the first time shouldering their proper responsibilities in the field of education. It is an opportune moment for establishing that close co-operation which has been so signally lacking in the past. The relation of government towards mission schools has not seldom been marked by irritating interference, or by a patronizing attitude not less irritating. An exiguous grant-in-aid has been awarded on the result of annual examination tests on the recommendation of an inspector of the board school type. The government has perhaps carried on one or two secondary schools, and in order to afford educational opportunities for the Moslem section of the population has established various Mohammedan schools.

This phase of educational development came to an end in Nigeria, as in the rest of Africa under British control, with the publication in 1925 by the Colonial Office of the Memorandum, *Educational Policy in British Tropical Africa,** the first of a series of policy statements consequential upon the setting up of the Advisory Committee on Native Education in British Tropical African Dependencies in 1923, and its successor, the Advisory Committee on Education in the Colonies, in 1929.

The Committee was a purely advisory body. The Secretary of State defined its duties in the following terms: "To advise the Secretary of State on any matters of Native Education in the British Colonies and Protectorates in Tropical Africa, which he may from time to time refer to them; and to assist him in advancing the progress of education in those Colonies and Protectorates."

* Advisory Committee on Native Education in British Tropical African Dependencies, *Education Policy in British Tropical Africa* (Cmd. 2347, HMSO, London, 1925).

In the Memorandum, which the Nigerian Government accepted as the basis of its own policy, the right to direct educational policy and to supervise all educational institutions by inspection or other means was reserved to the Government, whilst at the same time it was also laid down that voluntary effort be encouraged and advisory Boards of Education should be set up to ensure active co-operation of all concerned. The principle of adapting education to local conditions to the end that all sound elements in local tradition and social organization should be conserved whilst at the same time education should function as an instrument of progress and evolution was accepted. It was recognized that the material and economic development of the African dependencies side demanded a corresponding advance in the expenditure on education. It was still visualized that there would virtually be two systems—government and voluntary, but it was stated that schools run by voluntary agencies which attained a satisfactory standard of efficiency should be regarded as equally important in the scheme of education as those schools directly organized by the Government.

The Memorandum visualized the establishment of systems of education providing elementary, secondary, vocational, university and adult education. The latter was intended to provide means by which identity of outlook would be ensured between the newly educated generation and their parents.

Between 1925 and 1945 educational policy in Nigeria was based upon the principles enunciated in this and successive memoranda which increasingly related education to the social and economic development of the country. Following independence, the Federal and the Regional governments of Nigeria continued to use the technique of reports and memoranda produced by advisory bodies to elucidate principles of policy. This process of policy development may be regarded as having reached its apogee with the production in 1960 of the report of the commission on post-school certificate and higher education in Nigeria under the title *Investment in Education*.* The develop-

* See note on following page.

ment of education as a social institution responding to politics and economics and in turn influencing them is in essential the story of the years from 1925 to 1960.

* Commission on Post School Certificate and Higher Education in Nigeria (Sir Eric Ashby, Chairman), *Investment in Education* (Federal Ministry of Education, Lagos, 1960).

CHAPTER 4

DEVELOPMENT OF MODERN EDUCATION, 1926–1960

ONE of the first outcomes of the Phelps–Stokes Report and the Memorandum on Educational Policy in British Tropical Africa was the passing of a new Education Ordinance and Code which became effective on 26 May 1926; the Regulations under it became so on 1 September 1927. The provisions were restricted to the Colony and the southern provinces and were directed to the producing of orderly expansion of education. The main provisions included the keeping of a register of teachers; only persons enrolled on the register were to be permitted to teach in the schools in the Colony and the southern provinces. The Governor was given powers to be acted on with the advice of the Director of Education to control the opening of schools and to close schools deemed to be inefficient. The Board of Education was enlarged to include representatives of all the main bodies concerned with the provision of education in the hope that it would be able to offer advice of real benefit to the Government in the formulation of policy. The Ordinance also made provision for the voluntary agencies to appoint supervisors who were in effect inspectors to supervise the voluntary agency schools.

The Regulations made important changes in the system of making grants-in-aid. The efficiency of the schools was still the criteria on which grants were to be paid, but no longer would there be prescribed rules for assessing efficiency. Instead, inspectors were required to grade schools in overall terms into one of four categories, and grants were made payable on a related percentage of the total amount paid by the school in teachers' salaries. Minimum rates for the payment of teachers in assisted schools were laid down and the payment of captitation grants was discontinued. This latter step removed the temptation to accept pupils for admission regardless of the numbers and qualifications of the staff.

As a result of these changes in the legislation controlling the financing and supervision of education, the voluntary agencies concentrated their efforts on key schools, limited their work in the outlying districts and with the aid of the new supervisory service improved the quality of the teaching in the schools. In addition numbers of inefficient schools were closed and others given warning of the need for them to improve the quality of their work or suffer the same fate.

The 1926 Education Ordinance proved to be a landmark in the development of education in Nigeria in that it gave order and direction to its development and laid the foundation for a system. At the same time it provided the possibilities of systematically increasing the expenditure on education through the grants-in-aid system. Symptomatic of the change is the fact that whereas in 1923 out of the total revenue of the country £6,509,244, the expenditure on education was £100,063, or 1·5 per cent of the total revenue, from 1925 to 1929 it rose to nearly 5 per cent. In 1930, however, this trend of expanding expenditure on education went into reverse. Whereas in the estimates that year, £110,122 was provided for grants-in-aid to the voluntary agencies, in October of that year the Governor had to announce a cut to £85,000 which also represented the maximum grant to be available for the next three years. This reflected the impact of the world slump on the economics of Nigeria, and it also reflected the fact that education was still regarded as a spending service. The concept of education as an investment had yet to be formulated. The viewpoint of the Government was in direct contrast to that of the people, for despite the difficulties parents and guardians made such efforts to find school fees that in 1932 the Director of Education recorded in his annual report, "A proof of the widespread desire for education lies in the fact that one of the last economies of Southern Nigerian parents is in school

fees". The reaction of the voluntary agencies to the financial
stringency during these years was similar. In most cases teachers
accepted cuts in salaries and forewent the receipt of increments.
In some cases they accepted levies on the salaries in order to keep
schools going in the poorer areas. Even so, the school system
suffered seriously, many of the more able and best experienced
teachers drifted away from the profession, and the inspectorate
found it impossible to insist on the maintenance of the normal
standards of efficiency.

Despite the difficulties created by the world economic depres-
sion and the concept of education as a spending service, the
Director of Education, Mr. E. R. J. Hussey, put forward a
scheme for advance. In the Sessional Paper No. 31/1930 he
wrote:

> If we are now in a position to contemplate a gradual expansion of educa-
> tion during the next fifty or one hundred years which will permit not only
> a reasonable increase of school facilities for the masses but also of a
> gradually improving standard of higher education at the top, it is first
> necessary to determine what changes in the existing system will make such
> expansion possible. It is moreover advisable to make such changes as
> soon as is conveniently possible as every year's delay will make re-organi-
> zation more difficult.

In the proposals put forward by Mr. Hussey it was visualized
that education would be organized in three phases. The first
phase would consist of two years in an infant section and a further
four years, making six years of basic education in all with the
purpose of providing an education for life for the majority of the
pupils who would not go on to further formal education of any
kind whilst at the same time providing the first stage of education
for those who wished and were able to go further. The second or
intermediate stage of education was visualized as a six-year stage
after which a considerable proportion of the school leavers would
find employment, and a third stage would provide vocational
training "to provide well qualified assistants in medical, engineering and other vocations and teachers of higher middle schools".

Specific proposals were made for establishing training colleges
and middle schools under government control and the provision

of a translation bureau for work on the languages of instruction "so that not only will there be an ample supply of textbooks but also, in course of time, a large number of books for general reading".

Despite the difficulties both voluntary agencies and the Government carried out a certain amount of expansion, particularly in the provision of secondary schools and of teacher-training facilities. In an attempt to cater for the third stage of education as propounded by Mr. Hussey, Yaba Higher College was opened in February 1932 in temporary quarters in Lagos and moved to permanent quarters in 1934. Courses were provided in medicine, agriculture, engineering and in teacher-training at a higher level than was provided elsewhere in Nigeria. Initially, it was not intended to aim at courses of university level, the Governor, Sir Donald Cameron, at the opening ceremony in 1934 remarked: "As the level of attainment of students who matriculate at Yaba rises in proportion to the improvements in the schools from where these students come, the standard of the work at the College will rise in a corresponding degree, and we look forward to the time when it will be possible for men and women to obtain at Yaba external degrees of a British University."

A development of a different character, but one of considerable importance for the future, was the foundation of the Nigerian Union of Teachers. The Union, which was founded in 1930, aimed at bringing about professional unity among the teachers and getting for the profession a voice in the planning of education. By 1936 it had a membership of 667 teachers in eighteen affiliated branches with a representative on the Board of Education. The Union rapidly gained the confidence of the Education Department, a fact that is borne out by the frequent references in annual reports to its co-operation and helpfulness. The significance of the Union lies not only in its effectiveness in promoting its own interests but also in the fact that it demonstrated the capacity of the teachers to organize themselves successfully to undertake tasks different from those in which they had traditionally exercised their genius. The growth and strength of the Union owed much to the leadership of Mr. E. E. Esua, the first secretary.

Despite the efforts of the Government to give order and system to the provision of education, and despite the sacrifices made by parents and voluntary agencies, the demand for education greatly outstripped the funds available to meet that demand. The demand was not the artificial product of nationalist agitators, nor was it induced by official action on the part of either Government or missionaries. It was, without question, the genuine expression of a people who had come to realize in varying degree that their place in the changing world would be determined by the rate of educational advance and of the application of modern knowledge to their daily affairs. If for many this was still a matter of acquiring the magic of the white man's power through their schools, and if for many it was the key to individual economic and social development, it was for many also the means by which independence could be gained.

The discontent with the provision of education during this period has been described by Dr. Kenneth Dike, the first African Principal of the University of Ibadan in the following terms:

> The Nigerian discontent was concerned not so much with the contents of education. To a great extent the argument as to whether there should be more of industrial and technical than of literary education did not very much concern the majority of Nigerians. The overriding complaint was that there was not enough education—of any kind—for the masses of the people. The key to the understanding of the whole problem of education in Africa is the appreciation of the fact that the whole region thirsts for knowledge. The wealthy and the poor, the aristocrats and the lowest peasants, Christians, Moslems, and the "pagans", cry out for it. . . . Another aspect of the question is the fact that Africans believed, rightly or wrongly, that the kind of education offered under the British Colonial régime prepared them only for subordinate positions in all walks of life. . . . In nationalist parlance, therefore, Nigerians were being educated by the British overlords to fill the role of "hewers of wood and drawers of water". Even when a university institution was founded in the years 1930–1934, in the form of the Yaba Higher College, its graduates were rated inferior, in terms of salary and status, to graduates of British universities. . . . Of the first 181 graduates of the college, thirty-eight became either medical, agricultural, or forestry assistants; nineteen graduated as engineers, and six as surveyors. The rest were absorbed into educational, administrative,

and technical services as subordinate technicians and clerks. In short, the Yaba Higher College was attacked by Nigerian nationalists on many grounds and was never regarded by them as an adequate answer to their higher educational aspirations.*

In 1942 the first attempt was made by the Government to plan a way out of the impasse. In consultation with the voluntary agencies the Director of Education drew up a ten-year plan for educational development.† The plan was regarded with favour in Nigeria by those most intimately concerned with the provision of education because it held out the promise of ordered development, aimed at improving and stabilizing the terms and conditions of service of the non-government teachers, and gave education a place in the affairs of the Government it had never previously enjoyed. On the other hand, the plan was criticized strongly both in Nigeria and in the United Kingdom particularly because it appeared to touch but the fringe of the problem and this at estimated costs out of all proportion to the economics of the country as they then appeared and as they were interpreted in terms of policy. Two further criticisms made were that the plan having been prepared centrally, gave insufficient attention to provincial interests and that the statistical basis of the estimates was lacking in accuracy.

In so far as the plan was based upon a "shopping list" the criticism of its financial implications was fair, and the comment on the inadequacy of the statistical data on which the plan was based was equally valid. The criticism that provincial interests had been overlooked by the planners was less justifiable in that the voluntary agencies, who carried by far the greater responsibility for the general provision of education, based their advice upon the widest consultation. The much more serious weakness lay in the fact that none of the participants in the preparation of the plan had had any previous experience of such relatively long-term planning, nor was there any real appreciation of the need

---

* K. O. Dike, Development of modern education in Africa, ch. 12 in *The One and the Many* (Ed. J. N. Brookes, Harper, New York, 1962).
† *Nigeria: Ten Year Educational Plan* (Sessional Paper No. 6, 1944, Government Printer, Lagos, 1944).

to integrate educational, manpower and economic planning.

The plan was rejected by the Secretary of State who instructed the new Director of Education to re-examine the whole problem in the light of the comments of the Advisory Committee on Education in the Colonies to whom the plan had been submitted.

Although the education departments of the northern and southern provinces of the country were united in 1929, legislation continued to be enacted separately until the passing of the Education Ordinance of 1948 which made provision for the whole country. But educational development continued to be inhibited by the hostility of the emirs to Christian teaching and Western-type education. Furthermore, the viewpoint of Lugard that Christian ideas and Western education would militate against the success of his system of indirect rule, and that "the premature teaching of English inevitably leads to utter disrespect for British and native ideas alike, and to a denationalized and disorganized population" still influenced the thinking of many of the administrators. In consequence, by 1947 there were still only three secondary schools and just over 1100 primary schools in northern Nigeria as compared with forty-three secondary schools and nearly 5000 primary schools in the southern provinces. Not until 1950 did the responsible leaders of the north come to realize that it was necessary to build a sound and a widespread educational system to ensure that the north should attain a position in the rapidly developing Nigeria comparable with its size and population.

The first decisive step forward in the education programme during this period was taken in 1948 following the acceptance of the Asquith* and Elliot† Commissions reports by the United Kingdom Government. The Asquith Commission had been set up in August 1943 "To consider the principles which should guide the promotion of higher education, learning and research

* *Report of the Commission on Higher Education in the Colonies* (Cmd. 6647, HMSO London, 1945).
† *Report of the Commission on Higher Education in West Africa* (Cmd. 6655, HMSO, London, 1945).

and the development of universities in the Colonies; and to explore means whereby universities and other appropriate bodies in the United Kingdom may be able to co-operate with institutions in the Colonies in order to give effect to these principles". Two months previously a separate commission under the chairmanship of the Right Honourable Walter Elliot had been appointed "To report on the organization and facilities of the existing centres of higher education in British West Africa, and to make recommendations regarding future university development in that area". The reports of the two bodies, together with that of a third committee concerned with the provision of higher education in the West Indies, were published in June 1945.

The Elliot Commission Report contained the views of the majority as well as a minority report. Both groups, however, were agreed that a university college should be established in Nigeria. The Principal-Designate, Dr. Kenneth Mellanby, arrived in Nigeria in July 1947, and in January 1948 Yaba Higher College was transferred to Ibadan to form the nucleus of the new university college. The college operated under the scheme of Special Relationship with the University of London and also had the advantage of the services of the Inter-university Council for Higher Education in the Colonies (the title was later changed to that of the Inter-university Council for Higher Education Overseas).

Under the scheme of special relationship the college developed its own syllabuses and its own examinations, the University of London provided moderation through the appropriate boards of studies and special examination committees. The latter moderated the examination papers, marked the students' scripts independently of the college examiners and arrived at agreed pass-lists with them. This scheme ensured world-wide acceptance of the degrees and provided the college staff with the benefit of the accumulated experience of the University of London whilst permitting independence of action in the design of syllabuses and examination procedures. In similar way, the Inter-university Council put at the disposal of the college the joint experience of the United Kingdom universities and by helping in recruiting staff and forging links between the new institution and the old established universities. Furthermore, it provided advice to the United Kingdom Government about the allocation of financial aid to the university college from the Colonial Development and Welfare Funds.

The importance of this step is brought out when it is noted that from 1937 to 1945 only sixty-nine awards had been made by the Government to Nigerians to pursue degree studies in the United Kingdom. By comparison, 210 students were in residence at Ibadan in the academic year 1948–9, and in the intermediate examinations held in 1950—the first under special relationship— 19 out of 33 arts candidates, 61 out of 83 science candidates, and 7 out of 14 second M.B. examination candidates were success-ful. By 1960 the commission appointed by the Federal Ministry of Education, Nigeria, to investigate Nigeria's needs in the field of post-school certificate and higher education over the next twenty years was able to record that the University College Ibadan had in little more than a decade "built itself not only a noble range of buildings but an academic dignity and reputation which have given it a place of high importance in Nigeria and a position of respect in Africa and the world outside".*

Important as was the establishment of the University College at Ibadan, in terms of general educational development even more important was the publication in 1947 of the *Memorandum on Educational Policy for Nigeria*† because it set out a reasoned policy for development in relation to the needs of the country as a whole, and was intended as a basis for discussion by everybody concerned with education in Nigeria. Whilst it is true that policy statements had been made in the past and had been debated in the Legislative Council, and whilst it is also true that matters of policy were placed on the agenda of meetings of the Board of

* *Investment in Education: Report of the Commission on Post-school Certificate and Higher Education in Nigeria* (Federal Ministry of Education, Lagos, 1960).
† *Memorandum on Educational Policy in Nigeria* (Sessional Paper No. 20 of 1947, Government Printer, Lagos, 1947).

Education and of local education committees, these discussions had been confined almost entirely to official and professional interests. In the foreword to the Memorandum the comment is made: "It must not therefore be assumed that all the details of the policy set out in this memorandum have been irrevocably decided without the opportunity being given for full discussion by all concerned." The inclusion of this remark in the foreword is indicative of the change in attitude that had taken place. In 1925 the responsibility of Government for education had been enunciated as a first principle, co-operation and consultation with voluntary agencies had also been laid down as part of official policy. In practice consultation and co-operation had been limited almost entirely to government officials and representatives of the interested missions.

The keynote of the memorandum was that "Increased educational facilities cannot be provided with advantage except with the active co-operation of the communities concerned. The stage has been reached at which popular education will cease to be popular unless the communities concerned have a measure of control: and popular share in the control depends on the creation of some machinery of local government." It was recommended that Education Committees should be established with the intention that they should become committees of "Local Education Authorities" in the technical sense of the term. It was also proposed that responsibility in respect of primary education should be entrusted to these bodies and that in time they should develop into administrative bodies. Whilst this represented a big step forward, it was a step still marked by the spirit of parentalism as is clearly shown by the proviso with which the opening paragraph on local education authorities ends: "Such a development will require careful watching and the gradual delegation of administrative functions will depend on the extent to which these bodies can accept responsibility."

Another direction in which the Memorandum demonstrated a new attitude was in the standpoint taken about the financing of educational development. The Advisory Committee on Education in the Colonies had enunciated the view that a distinction should be made between: "(a) limitable commitments, namely, those to which a term can be set without harm to the nature of the service and with a reasonable assumption that the Territory will in due course be able to maintain or dispense with it and (b) non-limitable commitments, namely, those whose cost cannot be limited without fundamental harm to the nature of the service, and which must for their own security be developed within local resources." The importance of this principle has been borne out in a number of countries where projects good in themselves were started with the assistance of Colonial Development and Welfare Funds on the principle of "priming the pump" but with insufficient attention to the continuing costs of the projects. Linked with this approach to the financial implications of a development programme for education was the concern to dispel the idea that "Nigeria has a right to ask and the British taxpayer a duty to provide service without reference to local ability to support them. Acceptance of this idea militates against those qualities of independence, self respect, willingness to accept responsibility and initiative and judgement in carrying it out which are prerequisites to self-government."

Whilst the deeper significance of the relationship between education and social and economic development, which now dominates thinking about educational planning, had not been grasped when the Memorandum was written one paragraph in it suggests some appreciation of the relationship.

> The failure on the part of certain Colonial Governments to realize the true value of a properly conceived and developed education is reflected in many ways all of which contribute to impeding rather than helping its progress. For instance the financial policy usually balances the apparent material gains on the output of professionally trained men and women against the expenditure involved. Again, the importance of research work is not understood and the scope of the duties of the academic staffs is too narrowly defined.

By comparison with the views now becoming prevalent, these reflections on the financial aspects of educational development were but the first indications of a new way of looking at education.

Nevertheless, they were important precursors for the future, and all the more important in that they were enunciated at a time when political independence was still considered to be a long way off. One result of this was that when political independence did come there was already in existence a conceptual framework concerning education and its financing which made the planning of accelerated development easier than it might otherwise have been.

At the same time as the Memorandum was under preparation an exhaustive inquiry was being made by Mr. S. (later Sir Sidney) Phillipson, assisted by Mr. W. E. Holt, into the system of grants-in-aid of education. The Report*, which was published in 1948, offered an exposition of the problems and suggested four principles as the basis of a scheme for financing primary schools which had a validity far beyond Nigeria. The principles were that (1) grants-in-aid should be directed to facilitating balanced development of the whole primary system by ensuring a satisfactory balance between the senior and primary parts; (2) that there should be a division of cost between the public revenues and the localities served; (3) there should be zonal adjustment of the local contributions; and (4) the commitments of approved voluntary agencies should be defined at fixed intervals.

As has already been described, grants-in-aid from government funds had been given previously to only a small number of schools considered to be efficient and therefore placed on the list of approved schools. The Phillipson Report accepted the primary education system conducted by the voluntary agencies and the Native Administrations as part of a national system. The school was made the unit for calculating the grant-in-aid, and the financial assistance given was recognized as meeting an essential need and not a matter of privilege. It also sought to relate the primary school system to the secondary and higher education in such a way that through grants-in-aid the development of a

* *Grants in Aid of Education in Nigeria. A Review, with Recommendations* (Sessional Paper No. 8 of 1948, Government Printer, Lagos, 1948).

balanced system would be assured. In effect, the suggestions amounted to assuming primary education as a national responsibility with the ultimate objective of establishing a universal, compulsory and free system up to and including secondary education, the cost being shared between the Government and the local authorities through taxation and local rates.

The practical outcome of these two reports was the passing of a new Educational Ordinance which was to provide the machinery for carrying out the planned development of education for the next decade.

At the end of the decade, 1948–58, over 2,500,000 children were attending some 17,000 schools, there were over 25,000 students enrolled in the teacher-training colleges and more than 1800 students pursuing higher education in the Nigerian College of Arts, Science and Technology and the University College Ibadan, and something of the order of 1000 Nigerians were attending colleges and universities overseas. The total recurrent expenditure on education was of the order of £20 million, of which approximately £18 million came from Federal and Regional Government revenues.

On the face of things this represented a remarkable achievement, and, indeed, it was. Even so, the provisions made were deficient at every level, and there was an imbalance between the facilities for primary, secondary and post-secondary education as well as a lack of balance in the geographical distribution of schools and colleges as between the three regions.

The Western and Eastern Regions on achieving internal political independence had made great efforts to provide universal primary education on which they spent two-thirds of their regional education votes. The latter were between 30 and 40 per cent of the total regional budgets.

The inadequacies of the educational system were fully revealed in 1960 when the Report of the Commission on Post-school Certificate and Higher Education in Nigeria was published. The Commission had been set up by the Federal Government "to conduct an investigation into Nigeria's needs in the field of

Post-school Certificate and Higher Education over the next twenty years". The Commission consisted of three Nigerians, three Americans and three British. The Report is commonly referred to as the Ashby Report after the chairman of the Commission, Sir Eric Ashby.

The international character of the membership of the Commission was significant in that it indicated a change that had taken place in the attitude of the people of Nigeria. Whilst recognizing the special contribution that had been made by the British to the development of education, as an independent country, Nigeria's leaders recognized that educational experience other than British could be of value to them. But much more significant was the approach of the Commission to their brief. As in the case of the Elliot Commission in 1944, the Ashby Commission approached their task within the context of the whole education system but they set the system itself within a new framework by emphasizing the importance of taking into consideration the "consumer needs" for manpower and by insisting that education should be examined in relation to the aspirations of the nation for rapid social and economic progress. In respect of the latter they stated, "Our task is to forecast Nigeria's educational needs up to 1980. We could have approached this task by calculating what the country can afford to spend on education, and by proposing cautious, modest, and reasonable ways in which the educational system might be improved within the limits of the budget. We have unanimously rejected this approach to our task."* By adopting this viewpoint the Commission were making explicit a general complete change of attitude towards the financing of education. The view that expenditure on education should be limited to what could be afforded out of current resources, a view which had dominated the financial policy throughout the period of colonial tutelage, except for the "priming of the pump" policy of the Colonial Welfare and Development Acts, was therefore replaced by the

* *Investment in Education: Report of the Commission on Post-school Certificate and Higher Education in Nigeria* (Federal Ministry of Education, Lagos, 1960).

view that expenditure on education was in fact investment, a view which gave rise to the title of the report, *Investment in Education.*

The approach to their task was based upon the concept that by 1980 Nigeria would be

> a nation of some 50 million people, with industries, oil, and a well-developed agriculture; intimately associated with other free African countries on either side of its borders; a voice to be listened to in the Christian and the Moslem worlds; with its traditions in art preserved and fostered and with the beginnings of its own literature; a nation which is taking its place in technological civilization, with its own airways, its organs of mass communication, its research institutes.

In adhering to this assumption the members of the Commission were attempting to avoid the error of underestimating the pace at which West Africa was growing up, an error which had been characteristic of previous appraisals. Yet, in one respect, they were themselves already in error; the population census of 1963 produced a population figure of 55 million people, a figure of the order of which they had calculated would be the population at the end-point of their planning period. This but serves to underline the difficulty of long-term planning and of making projections, a weakness which Nigeria and similarly placed countries will have to contend with until adequate machinery exists for collecting and processing the necessary statistical data.

This weakness was, however, clearly recognized by the Commission. Professor Frederick Harbison, the member of the Commission responsible for the sections of the Report dealing with manpower makes the comment: "no attempt has been made to predict what the number of persons in the high-level manpower category is likely to be in the next decade. Nor is this Report a manpower survey, because as yet the statistical information is lacking for such a survey. This report merely suggests *minimum high-level manpower targets* for the period 1960–1970."

The third consideration which influenced the Commission in their findings was the capacity of the education system as they found it when they carried out their investigation. In terms of planning for the future they had to report that "under the present educational system more than half of the people already born, who would be part of the Nigeria of 1980, will never go to school". To remedy this situation would be a stupendous undertaking. But quantitative aspects of the task represented only one side of the coin. There was in addition the question of the quality of the education provided in the existing system to be considered. Nearly three-quarters of the teachers employed in the primary schools were untrained, and of those who were trained, two-thirds had received no more than a primary education before receiving professional training themselves.

In the secondary schools the inadequacies were equally serious, 3470 of the teachers engaged in secondary schools in 1958 out of a total of 4378 were neither graduates nor certificated teachers. The deficiencies were not limited to the quality of the teachers. Whereas the intake in the first year of the primary school in 1958 was 648,748 pupils, the intake for the first year of the secondary school was only 12,344, and there were only 553 pupils in the whole country taking sixth-form studies and therefore providing the potential recruitment for higher education. Even allowing for the fact that several thousand Nigerians attempted to qualify for higher education by private study and that of over 1000 Nigerians qualified for admission to the university, places were available at Ibadan for only about 300 of them. Even making allowance for the 800 or so Nigerians who in one way or another succeeded in gaining admission to universities overseas, there were many others who believed themselves to be unjustifiably deprived of the right to further education and reluctantly accepted employment, often uncongenial, in the hope that by renewed efforts they might secure a university education. This situation led the Commission to make proposals which they described as "massive, expensive, and unconventional", and for which "the Nigerian people will have to forego other things they want so that every available penny is invested in education". But as the Commission went on to remark, "Even this will not be enough.

Countries outside Nigeria will have to be enlisted to help with men and money. Nigerian education must for a time become an international exercise." In this respect Nigeria is typical of the low-income countries, in that socially desirable targets for the provision of primary education are unattainable in the foreseeable future without a considerable measure of external aid.

In respect of primary education, the Commission was of the opinion that enough children were completing primary education to provide a sufficient flow of recruits to secondary education, but they pointed out that the distribution of the flow was very uneven, whereas in the Eastern and Western Regions the educational pyramid was very broad at the base due to the efforts that had been made to provide universal primary education, and contracted far too sharply, in the Northern Region the pyramid was too slender at all levels. As a guide to ways of correcting this situation, the Commission suggested that the development of the system should aim at (1) producing enough children with post-secondary education to satisfy the nation's high-level manpower needs, (2) providing a proper balance as between primary, secondary and post-secondary education, and (3) narrowing the gap between the educational provision in the Northern Region and other regions whilst avoiding an unbalanced system in the north. To this end they suggested that by 1970 of 1000 children entering the primary schools in the south, there should be provision for all of them to complete their primary education, whereas in the north they set the target of 250 out of 1000 or 25 per cent to complete senior primary schooling as compared with 90 out of 1000 in 1958. Their other important recommendation was that a great effort should be made to improve the standard of English everywhere.

At the secondary level, they suggested that the school intake should be increased from 12,000 in 1958 to over 30,000 by 1970, and of these some 3500 should be able to go on to sixth-form work. Opportunities for the latter, it was suggested, should be provided in existing secondary schools and in new "National High Schools" as well as by means of part-time courses in technical institutes. It was also recommended that the financing of the sixth-form work should be a charge on the Federal Government funds.

To improve the quality of teachers in relation to the development of education envisaged, the Commission suggested that by 1970 half of the teaching staff of the secondary schools, technical institutes and training colleges should be graduates and that the remainder should be well-qualified non-graduate teachers of a category the Commission referred to as "Grade I". In the primary schools, the target set was that one teacher in fifteen should be Grade I. This grade of teacher was defined as one who had satisfactorily completed a two-year post school certificate professional course of training. It was also proposed that the primary school teacher should be trained in colleges associated with university institutes of education. In order to bring about this change it was suggested that 1000 teachers already holding Grade II teaching certificates should be recruited for further training each year and that 2000 recruits should be found from the secondary schools.

The further in-service training of the teachers already employed in the schools was recognized as a matter of some urgency, and it was suggested that there should be inaugurated a regular programme of annual one-month vacation courses in English and other subjects, for which instructors should be recruited from overseas. The Commission also drew attention to the need to improve the terms and conditions of service of the Grade I teachers, and, by a vigorous public relations programme, to create greater respect for the teaching profession. In advocating these latter steps, the Commission were giving recognition to the changed status of the teacher within the community in Nigeria. Whereas under the old dispensation of colonial government and denominational control of education the Nigerian teacher was a part of a small hierarchy with a predictable career and a relatively high level of security and engaged in work which resulted in close identification with the local community, under the new dispensation of political independence the teacher suddenly found his occupation a bridge to other openings. In comparison with the majority of the population, even the poorly trained teacher possesses a level of literacy, skill in communication, understanding of the established order and of the machinery of bureaucracy that gave him exceptional potential mobility. This, coupled with the fact that teaching provided little opportunity to become independent or rich led many teachers to make the short step from being local scribe, informal welfare worker, and counsellor, to being politician, trade union leader, public or private bureaucrat in the changed power structure. In drawing attention to the need to improve the conditions of the Grade I teacher, the Commission were pointing to the bridge function the occupation of teacher had developed.

In making recommendations with reference to education at the primary and secondary levels, the Commission was mainly primarily concerned with the foundations necessary to provide a sufficient supply of recruits for higher education. What must be emphasized, however, is that by doing so, they were making the unity of the educational system clear.

When the Commission came to deal with one of the major issues of their brief, namely the provision of university education, they decided to take as their starting point Harbison's estimate of the need for high-level manpower. This he had put at an output of at least 2000 graduates a year from Nigerian universities. At the time of the investigation the output was about 300 graduates. Even with the addition of Nigerians who graduate outside the country, there was a shortfall of at least 1000 graduates a year. The Commission accepted Harbison's estimates whilst at the same time pointing out that even if the proposed expansion were reached and maintained for ten years there would still be fewer university graduates per thousand of the population in Nigeria than in Ghana and Egypt in 1958. Their main recommendations were that (1) higher education should be concentrated in university institutions providing degree courses suited to Nigerian needs rather than to link professional studies exclusively to the examinations of professional bodies, and (2) that Federal resources should be concentrated upon the three existing centres, Ibadan, the proposed university for Northern Nigeria and the proposed University of Nigeria, Nsukka, together with a new university at Lagos. The purpose of these proposals was to increase the university population of Nigeria from a little over 1000 to 7500 as the first objective and to pass the 10,000 mark by 1970. At the same time each region would be served by a university, though the Commission stressed that they should all be national in outlook and should avoid unnecessary duplication of courses.

The assumption made by the Commission that the University College, Ibadan, would be the university to serve the Western Region was not accepted by the Western Region Government and a fifth institution, the University of Ife, was legislated for by the Western Region before the Federal Government had time to give their considered views on the Report.

When Nigeria was made independent as part of the process of federalization, education had been made the responsibility of the regions except in respect of higher education. For this reason, the University College, Ibadan, and the Nigerian College of Arts, Science and Technology with its branches at Zaria, Enugu and Ibadan had been charges upon the Federal funds. Under the pressure of Regional interests, however, steps had already been taken in the regions to set up universities sponsored by the regional governments.

The Commission gave consideration to the problem of regional interests not only in respect of the political and geographical factors but also with due regard to the fact that universities have "bonds of loyalty not only to the country which supports them, but also to the international company of universities all over the world". They pointed out that universities must be insulated from "the hot and cold winds of politics" and that this required that the membership of the governing council, whilst being representatives of the public, must not be agents of sectional interests or of political parties. Furthermore, the council must have a secure income to be disbursed entirely at its own discretion. They pressed that councils of the universities should reflect the unity of Nigeria. To this end they suggested that regions should be equally represented on the council of each university. The Commission also pointed out that there should be a strong academic representation on the governing body, and advised the inclusion of one or two academics from overseas who by their experience would be helpful in guiding the new university "into decisions which would enhance its international prestige".

In order that the best use should be made of the funds available from Federal and other sources for university education it was proposed that a National Universities Commission should be set up by an Act of the Federal Parliament. The Commission would be empowered to examine proposals for the establishment of institutions of higher learning which required Federal support and to advise the Federal Government whether grants should be made. In addition, the Commission would in consultation with the universities initiate and consider plans for balanced development to ensure that the universities met the national needs, receive block grants from the Federal Government for allocation to the universities, collect, examine and publish information about university finance and give advice to the Federal Government or to the universities on matters of higher education in the national interest.

The purpose of these proposals was to provide an instrument that would at the same time ensure that the national interests in education were properly looked after whilst at the same time ensuring the autonomy and security of the universities.

The Federal Government on receipt of the Report consulted the four Ministries of Education, the professional educationists through the Joint Consultative Committee on Education, the Reference Committees on Secondary Education, Teacher Training and Technical Education. Representatives of the existing institutions of higher education and the Nigerian Union of Teachers also took part in the consultations.

As a result of the consultations the Federal Government accepted the Report as a sound analysis of the then current situation and also accepted the recommendations in principle as the basis for the development programme for the next ten years. The main area of disagreement was with the targets set on the basis of Professor Harbison's assessment of the manpower needs. Concerning the manpower estimates, in the Federal White Paper the comment is made, "The targets set, though large in comparison with the present achievements and facilities, are considered to be low when measured against the strong political urge to step up manpower development, and appraised against the background of international duties and obligations". The Government accepted the targets as minimal, a point that had been made about them by both Professor Harbison and the Commission, and expressed the intention to relate planning and implementation to the continued scrutiny of the high-level manpower supply and demand by the Inter-regional Manpower Board.

The acceptance of the Report meant committing the country to a capital expenditure of about £75 million for the period 1961–70 and recurrent costs by 1970 also of about £75 million, and to an educational effort more than three times greater than was already being made. As has already been described, the Commission had made clear that their programme would involve the people of Nigeria in great sacrifices. The reaction of the Federal Government was: "The Federal Government is confident that, despite the sacrifices entailed in tackling this vast programme of educational development, there will be a concerted effort on the part of all concerned—Governments, voluntary agencies, teachers and the people of Nigeria, backed by the goodwill and practical assistance of Nigeria's friends overseas."

In all this the Federal Government were reflecting a common feature in the underdeveloped countries that has its roots in the people's zealous faith in the efficacy of education to bring about their success in their release from the shackles of poverty, disease and ignorance. Coupled with this was an appreciation of the fact that the effort in education must be related to the development of other nation-building activities.

In addition to considering the problems of educational

development in the main sectors of the formal system, the Commission paid attention to the provision of technical and commercial education and agricultural education. In one respect the Commission showed less appreciation of the relationship between education and the social and economic environment of the country in the past than might have been expected of them. They suggested that the major reason for the failure to develop other forms of education than the conventional secondary school was due to the fact the first Western schooling brought to Nigeria was a literary education, and that "once civil rule was established the expatriate administrators were graduates, most of them graduates in arts. And so the literary tradition and the university degree have become indelible symbols of prestige in Nigeria, by contrast technology, agriculture, and other practical subjects, particularly at the sub-professional level, have not one esteem." Such a judgement is much too facile an interpretation of the facts. In the main lack of esteem for non-literary professional and vocational training, and the failure of a variety of projects in agricultural education and in the crafts was due to the absence of opportunity to practise them profitably. In the twenties and the thirties of this century, farm training and land settlement projects were started by both the Government of Nigeria and the voluntary agencies, the former under the auspices of the Department of Agriculture at Oyo in Western Nigeria, and the latter by the Church Missionary Society with the co-operation of the Methodist and Scottish Presbyterian Missions at Asaba in Eastern Nigeria. The projects failed largely because there was no significant economic future for the young men on completion of their training, but at a deeper level they failed because they were designed without paying attention to the interrelationship between the training of people for their employment and the market for their skills and products. The projects directly run by Government suffered by the frequent changes in staff, and in some cases their demise was directly due to this. In the case of craftsmen, the attempts made at improving skills and techniques, as, for instance, in the case of a carpenter training scheme, established in Lagos in the twenties failed because there was not enough local demand for the quality of products made by the men after they had been trained. As for drift from the farm and the village to the towns, which was reported to the Commission and the difficulty of persuading "bright youngsters to enter the agricultural schools", the fact that except for a few who might gain employment in the Agricultural Department neither peasant farming nor the market prospects held out promise of economic success.

The closeness of the relationship between educational provision and economic and social improvement for the individual must be recognized if planned development is to succeed. In Nigeria, as in all countries, the social and political pressures for education are largely motivated by economic considerations. If the educational system fails to prepare people for the available jobs it is clearly in a state of imbalance, as a social institution. The successes and failures of projects for vocational education in Nigeria were directly related to the social and economic circumstances of the time. It is likely that the approach to vocational education will continue to prove inadequate at all levels unless this relationship is fully respected in its proper perspective in historical terms and also due regard is paid to the future pattern of industrialization.

One of the major difficulties at the present time, as it has been in the past, in the planning of vocational training is the lack of information. The Federal Advisory Committee on Technical Education and Industrial Training in 1959 had to record: "Our task has been complicated by the lack of detailed information concerning training requirements of some of the employers. . . . It appears that a number of employers are unable or reluctant to plan ahead for their training needs and have submitted figures without much thought or consideration to future development. Some employers failed to make any return."* In consequence of this, planning of vocational education and training as enunciated

* *Report of the Federal Advisory Committee on Technical Education and Industrial Training* (Federal Government Printer, Lagos, 1959).

in the various reports and proposals published is still being expressed in general terms of establishing different types of vocational and training institutions rather than in specific real targets. Alternatively, they are directed to specific individual projects without reference to the education system or the economy as a whole. This situation will not change until the Federal and Regional Manpower Boards are able to provide reasonably acceptable estimates of demands both in the public and the private sectors of industry, commerce and administration and in public service.

Two other considerations must be kept in mind when reflecting upon the provision of technical and vocational education throughout this period. The first is the fact that both commercial and government organizations requiring the services of a labour force with varying kinds of skill followed the tradition of the craft industries in Britain with some form of apprenticeship or on the job training. Secondly, the demand for workers with a high degree of advanced technical and theoretical knowledge was and still is comparatively small. Furthermore, such industrial development as is likely to take place will call for training for adaptation to changing skill needs rather than for the specialized crafts where a man once having learnt his craft will practise that craft alone for a lifetime.

Yet the network of vocational and technical training so far developed, consisting of post-primary trade centres, technical institutes and an engineering faculty in one of the universities is still geared essentially to the methods and content of a system established in Britain in the nineteenth century. Something of this problem has been recognized in recent investigations into technical and vocational education made in both the Eastern and the Western Regions.

The Commission appointed to review the educational system of Western Nigeria in December 1960 commenting upon the work they saw in the trade centres, of which there were then two for boys and one for girls, said: "It is particularly important that there should be long-term planning . . . for in the existing trade centres boys are being prepared for work which is becoming less common and even very difficult to find, because of changes in industrial methods."* Whilst Mr. Michael Goldway, who was responsible for the report on vocational education in Eastern Nigeria in 1961 pointed out that

> Nigeria's industrial development, in order to be both competitive at home and in world markets, should by-pass the technological evolution which characterized industrialized countries. . . . Fifty years ago, there was a clear-cut distinction between skilled and unskilled jobs in most industries. The skilled worker was then dealing with a rather limited range of machinery and raw materials and unskilled work could be done with no training at all. Today the situation is very different. . . . The skills which go into the making of a product have been shifted from the shop floor to preparatory stages. The work is now done by technicians—draftsmen, production planning, development engineers, metallurgists, etc. These are the skilled occupations of today. There is still a limited demand for the old type of craftsman, but it is slowly disappearing. Mechanization and handling devices have reduced the need for unskilled labour.†

Looked at in these terms, the present inadequacy in the facilities for technical and vocational education in Nigeria could be a blessing in disguise. For, given the right information about the pattern of industrial and economic development, it should be possible for the expansion of vocational and technical education to be forward-looking and to be geared to future demands. In this respect it is of some significance that commenting upon the twenty-four technical and vocational institutions in existence in Eastern Nigeria, of which two were financed and run by Government, one government subsidized and the rest unaided, Mr. Goldway said: "Among those institutions only seven are of importance". And of those seven, those run within industry, namely the Shell–BP school at Port Harcourt and the United African Trading Company schools for motor-mechanics at Enugu and Aba, were specially well equipped and provided excellent training. This is a point which serves to emphasize the need for

* *Report of the Commission Appointed to Review the Educational System of Western Nigeria* (Government Printer, Ibadan, 1961).
† M. Goldway, *Report on Investigation of Vocational Education in Eastern Nigeria* (Ministry of Education Eastern Nigeria, Official Document No. 13, of 1961, Enugu, 1961).

the closest co-operation between industry and Government.
Industrial concerns in their own interests are likely to be well
aware of the best levels and methods of training that are relevant
to their current and future needs. The point is further made from
a different point of view in the comments on some of the vocational schools set up by private initiative which left much to be
desired. One of the reasons why the voluntary agencies have
played, comparatively speaking, so small a part in developing
technical education is due to the fact that it is one of the most
expensive forms of education. And though every encouragement
should be given to private initiative it will be necessary for
Government to exercise supervision over such efforts and be
prepared to give grants towards the equipment of workshops and
laboratories where the private initiative can be integrated into
the planned development of technical and vocational education.
The foreseeable pattern of development of the economy of
Nigeria suggests, however, that the major responsibility for the
development of technical and vocational education must lie
with Government and industry directly.

One aspect of vocational training to which attention has been
given over a long period with not very satisfactory results is in
agriculture. Apart from the efforts of the voluntary agencies to
make farming a part of the training of teachers in the training
colleges, and the efforts already referred to, to train primary
school leavers for land settlement at Oyo and Asaba, the Department of Education, in 1937, inaugurated courses at Ibadan for
trained teachers in school farming methods, rural science,
hygiene, economics and other related subjects. Later a similar
centre was opened at Umuahia. The object of these centres was to
give the rural schools specialist staff capable of giving instruction
in rural science and elementary farming methods based upon
experience accumulated by the Agricultural Department. The
work attracted attention outside the country, and thanks to a
long period of continuity of direction by Mr. Herrington, the
officer originally put in charge of the development, the content
and the methods of teaching were systematically modified in the

light of experience as well as in the light of practice elsewhere. Despite the quality and the persistence of this effort in 1961 the Federal Government in the White Paper on Educational Development, 1961–70, Sessional Paper No. 3 of 1961, expressed its perturbation about "the existing state of agricultural education and the dearth of Nigerian recruits into the agricultural services"

In this sector of the life of the community more than in any other the relation between education and the social and economic conditions is clear. Whilst the Federal Government recognized the need for making the terms and conditions of service more attractive in order to safeguard what is and will be for a long time to come, the mainstay of the country's economy, the Western Region Government in its plan for Regional Development defined the impediments to the development of an efficient agricultural system. These were (1) land tenure problems, (2) problems of fragmented holdings, (3) lack of capital, (4) poor farming techniques, (5) lack of storage facilities, and (6) inefficient distribution and marketing. Only one of these impediments, namely poor farming techniques is directly susceptible to treatment in educational terms, though all the other impediments, in addition to legislative and economic or technical treatment also involve educational action through extension methods in order to gain understanding co-operation from the adult members of the community.

In 1959 there was begun a scheme of training and land settlement that echoes the abortive experiment of the thirties in the Oyo Province. But there is one major improvement which could make all the difference. That is in addition to providing training, long-term credit is made available to the successful trainees selected to take part in the farm settlements. The essential features of the scheme are the training of selected young men and their establishment on holdings in groups of 200 on land settlement units of 4000–6000 acres under the direction of field staff of the Ministry of Agriculture and Natural Resources. Each land settlement unit will have certain common services and amenities, the settlers being provided with credit facilities repayable over a period of fifteen years. The object of this project is to show that farming can be both a profitable and an attractive way of life. The economic, social and the educational aspects of the problem are integrated, and it is in this respect that the approach differs from that of the previous attempts to tackle the educational problems of agriculture.

The programme was begun with thirteen settlements, a further group of fourteen were started in 1962–3, and a third group of eight are scheduled to be started in the financial year 1964–5. The first group of settlers left the Farm Institute in January 1963. Economic production is expected to start in 1965–6, and it is expected that 600 holdings will be in full production by 1970–1. The expenditure involved for the period ending 1965–6 is estimated to amount to £2,700,000. This is a programme in which, as has already been said, the social, economic and educational factors have been integrated. But it is little more than a large-scale demonstration project. Of the value of the impact of the project upon the overall agricultural development of the Region there is no doubt, but the relatively high cost of the project is a matter of some concern. In addition to providing two years of training for the selected settlers, however, the farm institutes also give courses to other young farmers, and in all approximately 500 trained young men will be produced each year under the scheme. A similar scheme on a more modest scale is being developed in the Eastern Region.

The combination of agricultural training and land settlement now being developed is an example of the way in which education and economic planning needs to be linked. Some of the people concerned with the missionary enterprises of the last century had some appreciation of this interrelationship, as, for instance, the founders of the Hope Waddell Institution at Calabar. Therefore, in one sense the educational story has turned full circle, in another sense the country may be seen as having arrived at the general goal prescribed in the 1925 Memorandum on Education in British Tropical Africa, namely a complete system of education from infancy to adulthood. The filling out of the system and the adjustment of its contents and methods to the changing needs of the future represents the major tasks that lie ahead. Before considering the future, however, three other aspects of the development of education must be given some attention. Except for minor references, little comment has been made upon the content and methodology of the education provided, no reference has been made to the ancillary educational services, and the subject of external aid has hardly been mentioned.

CHAPTER 5

THE CONTENT AND METHODOLOGY OF EDUCATION

THE literature on education in Nigeria abounds with adverse criticisms of the content. In this, Nigeria resembles every other African country. Following their study of education in Africa in 1920–1, the African Education Commission, set up under the auspices of the Phelps–Stokes Fund, and which included three missionaries in its membership, commented upon the kind of education they found, in the following terms:

> though educational facilities in Africa are largely credited to missions and a really great service has been rendered by them to the Native people, many of the missions have yet to realize the full significance of education in the development of the African people. The defects in the educational program, so far as they exist, have usually been due to their conception of education. Some have thought of education merely as the imparting of information, or, at most, as the development of the mind without relation to moral and spiritual life. Others have thought of education merely as necessary chiefly to enable the Natives to read the Bible and to understand the spirit of Christianity. This group has been content with education in books. For the masses they have provided the three R's. For the catechists and advanced pupils they have endeavoured to give a knowledge of literature, including, of course, an interpretation of religion. In this limiting education to classroom instruction in books, missionaries were following the ideals prevailing in their home country.*

The last sentence of this comment contains the key to the problem. In so far as the missionaries were concerned with education they had but one pattern to follow, namely that with which they were familiar from their own experience. The extent to which this was so is reflected in the titles given to institutions, quite apart from what was taught and how it was taught. The first secondary school established in Nigeria by the Church

* L. J. Lewis (Ed.), *Phelps–Stokes Reports on Education in Africa (Abridged)* (Oxford University Press, London, 1962), p. 9.

Missionary Society was the CMS *grammar* school, the secondary school established by the American Baptist Missionary Society, was called the Baptist *academy*.

The Phelps–Stokes Commissions advocated a policy of adaptation of education to the environment, and as their brief had required them, they did so in the light of the religious, social, hygienic and economic conditions. Their advice was taken into account by the committee responsible for producing the Memorandum on Educational Policy in British Tropical Africa which was accepted by the Nigerian Government as the basis for developing its own policy.

Two of the principles laid down in the Memorandum were taken note of by both Government and missionary education authorities. In the first principle to be noted it was maintained that education should be adapted to local conditions in such a way as would enable it to conserve all sound elements in local tradition and social organization, while at the same time should function as an instrument of progress and evolution. Between 1925 and the outbreak of the Second World War a number of projects were launched to give effect to this principle. In Northern Nigeria, for example, courses organized for visiting teachers at Toro and Gombé* attempted to provide guidance and leadership to the teachers in relating the work of the school to the life of the community. Those taking part in the courses were chosen from experienced teachers, both trained and untrained, who had shown initiative and energy in their work, and who had set a personal example to their colleagues and the local community by their endeavours and qualities of leadership.

Living quarters were provided for the students in normal village buildings and the men were able to bring their families with them to the training course. They made their own domestic arrangements and were *in statu pupillari* during formal working hours only.

* P. G. S. Baylis, *Report on a Course for the Training of Visiting Teachers held at Togo Gombé, Northern Provinces of Nigeria, 1936–38* (Colonial 174, HMSO, London, 1940).

The first part of the course, lasting eight months, consisted of practical work in mixed farming, dry-season gardening, health and hygiene, first-aid, carpentry, crafts and building, together with the study of school organization and management. This was followed by an eight-month period which they spent in their own provinces to widen their experience. During this period they lived in groups in selected villages for periods of a few weeks at a time. Teaching in schools alternated with short intervals at the centre for discussion, correction of written work, further instruction and the preparation of programmes for the next visit. In addition to their work in the schools, the participants in the courses gained first-hand knowledge of the problems of community service by working with groups of adults, and by assisting in the formation of parents' committees which they attended in an advisory capacity.

At Omu in the Ilorin Province of Northern Nigeria an attempt was made to pattern the life and activities of the school upon local economic and social conditions in such a way as "to combat the subversive tendencies which were troubling the minds of the older men and guide the inevitable changes so that they might benefit the people".* In working out the organization and activities of the school the rural character of the community served was given careful thought and the time-table provided for a strong bias towards agriculture and manual work. The community was largely a Moslem one, and the school was under the management of a Moslem administration. So the provision for moral instruction and religious practice was orientated towards Islam, but separate provision was made for the religious instruction of the pupils who came from Christian families.

Relating the training of girls to local conditions and needs was also a matter of imaginative experiment. At Akure, the Church Missionary Society had established a training centre for girls which aimed at preparing them for marriage. For the most part the girls admitted to the course were fiancées or wives of teachers

* J. D. Clarke, *Omu: An African Experiment in Education* (Longmans, London, 1937), p. 7.

and catechists in training. The course was intended to give the young women a preparation both for marriage and for sharing community leadership with their husbands. In 1937 the work of this centre was extended, and with the aid of the students, the staff organized a three-week course in the Kukuruku district for illiterate women. The instruction was limited to aspects of domestic science and hygiene related to the circumstances in which the people lived. A similar project was developed at a training centre for women organized by the Methodist Missionary Society at Ilesha.

In Northern Nigeria in 1928, at a conference held at Katsina, the question of the status of the teacher as a member of the community was discussed. It was reported that the Chief Instructor of the crafts school at Maiduguri had been given by the Shehu the title of "mala", that is, Head of the Blacksmiths' Guild, and his local prestige had been raised thereby. At Yola the head teacher of the primary school had been publicly invested by the Lamidu with the title of "mukadaami" which raised his dignity among the mallams of the emirate. The importance of these events lay in the recognition given to the teachers in the alien education system; they were accepted as persons of distinction in the local society. The Conference welcomed the spontaneous conferring of the title by emirs but deprecated the idea that either the Resident of the Province or the Director of Education should be responsible for making any proposals for action of this kind.

At a different educational level, the conference concerned itself with the training of kadis and showed themselves to be interested in the problem of relating education to the social circumstances. In a paper submitted to the conference by the Lieutenant Governor, he had this to say:

> At present our Education Department has little effect on the minds of the 12,000,000 natives whom nominally it is its function to mould, and whom some day it will mould, though the moulding period will always be comparatively brief in the span of life. Of these potential pupils 67 per cent are Moslems, and however young the boys and girls are who come to school their minds will be already moulded by certain early influences to

which they will be subject for most of the rest of their lives, i.e. Islamic influences.*

The beliefs, ethics and the universal code of conduct which formed the basis of the influences referred to are all enshrined in the Qur'an and in the Sunna or tradition of Mohammed's life, action and sayings. From these two sources Moslem Jurists and Divines have deducted the whole corpus of law and approved practice which is called the Sharia. The Kadi (Alkali) is the local interpreter of the sacred law and practice, and as such, the Lieutenant Governor saw him as "in a sense the arbiter who says whether the teaching of the Education Officer is good or bad, pious or impious, useful or useless". He saw the key to the educational situation to be the Kadi, or in the plural, Ulema.

> If the Kadi and Ulema are of a liberal mind and receptive type we shall find it much easier to make headway with moulding the young people who must look up to them and their opinion. . . . From the point of view of an Education Department, therefore, the training of Alkalis is a subject which merits not only close attention, but departmental action, in the sense that the Department itself should supplement local endeavours. . . . It seems to me that the logical education from the premises, set forth above, is that some attempt to educate or influence the Ulema class, or some of them, should precede any comprehensive attempt to include the Koranic schools as a whole in our system.†

In making suggestions about how this might be done through recruiting "a kind of mallam class" for training, the best of them being selected to become kadis and the rest of them being trained as teachers for Qur'anic schools under government supervision and auspices, reference was made to the success which had accompanied such a plan at Maiduguri. There, the school and mallam classes had been brought together and harmonious co-operation had been established in place of jealousy and distrust.

When we turn to the actual content of the school syllabuses we find that despite the criticisms levelled at them they were, in

---

* J. D. Clarke, *Omu: An African Experiment in Education* (Longmans, London, 1937), p. 7.
† *Nigeria Northern Provinces, Education Conference, March 1928* (Government Printer, Kaduna, 1928), pp. 16–18.

fact, designed to relate the content to local circumstances to some extent.

In a Report submitted for the Imperial Education Conference, 1913, the programme of study in infant schools covering five classes, provided for instruction in the three R's, and nature study in the vernacular for the first three years, with English being introduced as a subject in the fourth year. In addition, provision for kindergarten activities was prescribed. In the primary schools, in addition to continuing instruction in the three R's, nature study, hygiene and sanitation, manual or agricultural training and moral instruction were compulsory subjects in all classes. The optional subjects were history, geography, physical exercises, singing, typewriting and shorthand. In girls' schools the compulsory subjects included domestic economy. Commenting upon the place of manual training the Report says: "Apart from its providing for a supply of skilled labourers and craftsmen to meet an ever-increasing demand consequent upon civilization, the betterment of the community, and the wants which are inevitably created by contact with European influences, there is the consideration of its effect as a factor in the building-up of character, and in inculcating the object lesson that manual work is no indignity."* After describing the provision made for the supervision of this aspect of the work of the school, the Report goes on to deal with the trade schools and the technical departments of secondary schools. The crafts which were provided for in government schools at Bonny and Warri were those of carpenter and cooper, at the Hope Waddell Institute of the United Free Church of Scotland, carpenter, tailor and printer. At the Onitsha Industrial Mission carpentering, cabinet making and building construction were taught. In terms of the current economy these provisions were realistic, being directly related to the employment opportunities then existing and as far as could be foreseen, likely to be available in the immediate future.

* *Imperial Education Conference Papers. III. Education Systems of the Chief Colonies not Possessing Responsible Government* (Southern Nigeria, HMSO, London, 1913).

At another level of technical training the Report contains references to the provision of technical scholarships in connection with Government Railways, Public Works, and Marine Departments. There were junior scholarships for candidates over 14 years of age, who were physically fit for mechanical work and who had passed the Standard VI requirements of the Education Code or a qualifying equivalent examination. Six senior scholarships tenable for three years at some engineering or railway works in the United Kingdom or Ceylon or the Straits Settlements. The holders were expected, on completion of their training to return to Government Service for a further period of three years.

In addition to these provisions there were evening classes organized for apprentices employed at the Public Works and Marine Departments.

At the secondary school level, the Report stated that education was in its infancy. A secondary school was defined as "a school or department of a school in which the subjects prescribed for such schools are taught, and for the proper teaching of which there is, in the opinion of the Director, of Education, an adequate staff". There were, in fact, eight such schools. Apart from the Hope Waddell Institute in the Eastern Province at Calabar, and the Abeokuta Grammar School, not then recognized by the Department of Education, all the secondary school provision was to be found in Lagos.

The object of the single government-sponsored school, King's College, "was to provide for the youth of the Colony a higher education than that supplied by the existing schools, to prepare them for the Matriculation examination of the University of London, and to give a useful course of study to those who intend to qualify for professional life or to enter Government or mercantile service". In addition to the normal school programme, the College held evening classes for apprentices, already referred to, for young men and women who wished to improve their general education, and for clerks requiring instruction in book-keeping and shorthand. These offerings were without question related to the interests and needs of a small but significant sector of the community. But in so far as the content of the syllabuses was prescribed by the examination requirements of the Cambridge Junior and Senior Local Examinations, and the Matriculation Examination of the University of London, and which did not at that time provide special papers based upon local material, the courses were hardly relevant to the local environment.

Adverse criticisms have been made of the contents of the syllabuses, in particular, to the emphasis upon British history and geography, and the approach based upon the rote learning of facts such as lists of the kings of England, names of rivers, mountains and their heights. But it must be noted that these criticisms were rarely accompanied by any constructive alternative proposals.

The first major contribution to the solution of this problem came in 1933 with the publication of *The Teachers' History and Geography Handbook* (for Standards (grades) 1 to 4). The general scheme of the geography syllabus was designed to give the child as clear an idea as possible of all that pertained to his own locality, some understanding of the differences between his own locality and the other main climatic regions of Nigeria and how the different environments influence the lives of the people living in them. In addition, the latter part of the syllabus was designed to give some understanding about the countries with which Nigeria was connected politically and economically, and how events in those countries might influence the lives of people in Nigeria.

In dealing with history, the syllabus for the first two years was concerned with local history to be discovered by direct inquiry into the foundation of the village or town. For Standards 3 and 4, the syllabus was given a more formal structure in the form of two parallel courses, one in elementary civics, and the other an outline study of the history of Nigeria. In suggesting methods of treatment, the author of the syllabus emphasized that the teacher should arrange his teaching to suit his own locality. "Thus while he is adding to his general knowledge of Nigerian history he should not neglect to collect illustrative detail for the various topics of the syllabus from the local history of town or village in which the school is situated."* In preparing the syllabus the author took notice of the fact that many teachers were untrained, "or at any rate untrained in the present syllabus, and that no textbooks are available which are entirely suitable" by including several chapters giving information about the various sections of the syllabus. In the preface, reference is made to three sources of local information. Unfortunately, they were references that might have been available to administrative officers and senior education officers, but were far beyond the purses of the teachers.

At another level, the author of this syllabus made a further contribution to the idea of relating what should be taught to the local environment, in the form of a history course for the upper levels of the primary school and the junior levels of the secondary school entitled *Tropical Africa in World History*. This was an attempt to give a view of world history from inside the continent. At the time, it represented a great step forward, and the fact that it is still widely used, is some evidence of its continuing relevance to local needs, though it might also be regarded as evidence of the conservatism of the teachers.

Reference has been made to the fact that secondary education was tied to external examinations and that the syllabus requirements of these examinations were not related to local conditions. With emphasis given to the need to relate education to the local environment which sprang from the acceptance of the principles set out in the 1925 Memorandum on Educational Policy in Tropical Africa the modification of syllabus requirements received attention anew. One of the more interesting experiments was carried out at King's College, Lagos, where a science syllabus specially designed to meet local conditions was adopted with the co-operation of the Cambridge Schools Examinations Syndicate. This was possible because the Cambridge Syndicate Examination regulations allowed the acceptance of special syllabuses provided that it could be demonstrated that there were teachers qualified

* T. R. Batten, *The Teachers' History and Geography Handbook* (CMS, Lagos, 5th edition, 1944), p. 235.

to teach the proposed subject-matter, that suitable materials and equipment were available for the study of the subject along the lines prescribed, that examiners were available, and that the content of the syllabus could be equated to the standard syllabuses for the subject. In addition, certain of the Nigerian languages were accepted for study and examination at the School Certificate and London Matriculation level. In history and geography relatively minor but nonetheless significant changes were also made which offered opportunity to relate studies more closely to local interests.

In addition to the difficulties of designing local syllabuses because of the lack of facts about the environment the majority of schools were further handicapped because they had little money to spend on equipment and materials. This particularly affected the mission secondary schools in their attempts to develop the teaching of science. In 1940, the then Inspector for Science teaching, Mr. E. H. Duckworth, calculated that to provide the apparatus necessary to teach physics to the school certificate examination requirements would have cost approximately £1000 per school. The alternative, was to attempt to teach the pupils with the help of the blackboard and pictures, and to depend upon the retentive memories of the pupils to be able to reproduce the facts in examinations. Science could be taught and was taught in this way successfully, if success was measurable by examination results. But the educational consequences were lamentable. In order to demonstrate that the problem could be overcome, Mr. Duckworth, with the co-operation of two locally trained science teachers on the staff of the CMS Grammar School, Lagos, carried out an experiment in making apparatus. At a cost of £100 for material and a mechanic's time over 700 pieces of apparatus were produced to cover nearly every section of the syllabus. In a final comment on the project, Mr. Duckworth remarked, "Education in West Africa will go on increasing, and the elementary schools will also require simple biological equipment. The idea of using models and specimens in teaching history and geography is just taking root and will make new demands on workshop activities. There is great scope ahead for a central workshop and individual school workshops."*

This descriptive catalogue of experiment and demonstration of enlightened and forward-looking educational work, is but a sample of what was going on in the schools and colleges. Yet, as late as 1961, the Commission appointed to review the educational system of Western Nigeria found it necessary to be extremely critical of the results achieved. In the forefront of their criticisms of the primary schools were the familiar themes that primary education alienates the child from its environment, and that rural primary school leavers migrate to the towns in search of pen-pushing jobs for which they are not trained. Whilst they found that on the whole the syllabus for nature study, gardening and health was satisfactorily related to local conditions, they recorded their opinion that, "There was very little sign of a development of lively curiosity and a desire to know about the immediate environment and the world outside. One got the impression that the pupils were just sponges imbibing knowledge not understood or digested, for the sole purpose of 'regurgitating' it for examinations." They did not find any wish to acquire practical skills, nor did they find respect for the value of manual work. They came to the conclusion that all the pupils wanted was to became junior clerks in offices. An interesting gloss on this is their remark, "We are told that some of the teachers use gardening as a form of punishment for the pupils". When they turned their attention to the secondary modern schools which had been inaugurated in 1955 to provide the key to vocational and professional training at the lower levels, they found it necessary to record a situation as depressing as they had found in the primary schools. The syllabus consisted of mathematics, nature study and biology, civics and history, geography, English and English literature, arts and crafts, rural science, woodwork and light metalwork, home economics, needlework, elementary book-keeping and elementary commerce. These syllabuses were

* E. H. Duckworth, *Science Apparatus Making in Nigeria, Oversea Education*, vol. xii, No. 1 (HMSO, London, 1940), p. 59.

detailed and well thought out. But the Commission had to report:

> Very few of the modern schools which we saw had adequate staff and few indeed offered any of the vocational courses. At the moment most of them only offer the purely academic course which provides only a "polishing" of the education received at the primary school. Some of them are beginning to offer commercial subjects, but none of the schools we saw had the equipment to do metal-work and wood-work and there was very little evidence of rural science and art and handicrafts.*

Their criticism of the secondary grammar schools was brief but devastating.

> The only serious criticism of the secondary grammar school is the neglect of any technical or practical education. At present secondary school boys seem to have been groomed to think of themselves as being too good for any sort of manual work. It was observed that even the science learnt is very much out-of-date laboratory science and not related to their environment or in keeping with modern scientific knowledge.†

Their remarks on the provisions for teacher-training suggested inadequacies similar to those they had found in the primary and secondary school courses.

This picture of frequent review of the objectives of education, the design of syllabuses to meet the objectives, imaginative experiment and attempts to provide suitable teaching materials related to the environment not resulting in progressive general improvement in the education provided is not unique to Nigeria. It is of the utmost importance that the causes of failure should be correctly diagnosed and suitable remedies be applied, if the tremendous financial effort of the people of Nigeria, and the very considerable amount of external aid for education are not too dissipated in fruitless or disappointing enterprises.

One obvious source of weakness lies in the teaching profession itself. It has been described as a "sick profession", and in some respects it is so. The minimum qualifications for entry into the profession are low. The traditional assumption that schools can

* *Report of the Commission Appointed to Review the Educational System of Western Nigeria* (Government Printer, Ibadan, 1961), pp. 4–8.
† *Report of the Commission Appointed to Review the Educational System of Western Nigeria* (Government Printer, Ibadan, 1961), pp. 4–8.

be run satisfactorily with a high proportion of untrained teachers whose academic attainments are no higher than those to which their pupils aspire has undoubtedly contributed to the low status of the profession. For those with qualifications the salary scales are not comparable with those of other types of employment, and the possibilities of promotion within the profession are comparatively limited. Many teachers are more concerned with getting better qualifications than with carrying out their duties efficiently, and many find it more remunerative to use their spare time in private coaching and cramming private pupils for examinations. The "bridge character" of the profession referred to earlier has become increasingly significant making it even easier and more tempting than in the past for teachers to leave the profession. The solution to this aspect of the problem is primarily one of finance, but money alone will not improve the quality of the education. There are other things to be done.

Part of the problem lies in design of the history and geography syllabuses for the primary schools, referred to earlier. When new syllabuses involving the use of new material and new methods of treatment are introduced not only have courses in the training colleges to be changed but teachers already in-service have to be re-equipped to deal with the new content and the new methods. The failure to make adequate and systematic provision for such in-service training is one of the most marked weaknesses of the past and, indeed, the present.

Until recently another factor contributory to the failure of the schools to benefit from successful experiments was the lack of effective means of rapidly disseminating information about the experiments and how the results were obtained. But, more frequently, failure to benefit from experiments was due to a defect in the organization of the colonial service itself. Not infrequently, the person responsible for the design of an experiment and its implementation would be moved to other work before the experiment could be completed. Or, alternatively, changes of duty did not permit of the appropriate follow-up. It might have been expected that with political independence, and the departure of the expatriate, a greater degree of stability within the profession would have been obtained. This, however, has not been so. Apart from the frequency of turnover of local personnel, the replacement of expatriates on a career service basis by expatriates on short-term contracts has increased the rate of turn-over of teachers and administrators. The need for continuity of staff as a necessary concomitant to successful development of syllabuses and teaching method has not been recognized, and until it is, there is little prospect of syllabuses, however good, being put into effect. This subject will be discussed further in the final chapter.

CHAPTER 6

ANCILLARY EDUCATION SERVICES

IN ADDITION to the formal educational system any society requires and in varying degree acquires ancillary educational services. In Nigeria, as elsewhere, the first of these services appeared in the form of newspaper and periodicals.

Apart from early commercial ventures in the publishing of newspapers in English, the missionary bodies produced their own magazines dealing with religious and parochial matters both in English and in vernacular languages. Training colleges and secondary schools produced magazines intended for the information of former pupils. By 1959 there were seventy-two newspapers and periodicals listed as being in regular circulation, the circulation being of the order of 700,000 copies. There were twenty-six different publications entirely in Nigerian languages with a circulation estimated at 285,000, and there were twelve published in English and one or more Nigerian languages, with a total circulation of 56,000. A monthly newspaper for children published in English had a circulation of 60,000.* In relation to the total population figures these figures are still pitifully small. Even so for the literate community they were a source of influence and information. There was a strongly didactic flavour in the policy of the founders of many of the papers, for instance, the first newspaper published in Hausa was given a Hausa title, which translated reads: "Truth is worth more than a penny." A very successful monthly published by the Church Missionary Society in Lagos carried the title, *In Leisure Hours*. One publication

* *Report on the Press in West Africa* (distributed by the Director, Department of Extra-mural Studies, University College, Ibadan, 1959), provides a detailed statistical analysis of the newspapers and magazines then in circulation in the context of a general survey.

of remarkable quality was and is the magazine *Nigeria*. This was initiated by Mr. E. H. Duckworth as a magazine of general interest. After producing it for a few years at his own expense the magazine was taken over by the Government, and has continued to provide a source of stimulating and informative articles about Nigeria with lavish illustrations of an exceptional high quality. The magazine produced by the Nigerian Field Society with its more specialist interest gave a service of equal quality and which incidentally provided teachers of biology with a trustworthy source of information about the flora and fauna of the country at a time when the only textbooks dealing with tropical plants and animals had to be obtained from publishers catering for India and Ceylon.

The existence of a local press based upon the production of newspapers and magazines has also contributed to other kinds of publications. The mission presses at Lagos, Port Harcourt and Jos, whilst intended primarily to serve the interests of the churches also provided a flow of informative ephemera of other kinds. The Gaskiya Corporation established at Zaria by the Government with initial assistance from the Colonial Welfare and Development Funds, in addition to printing newspapers in the vernaculars also published school textbooks in Hausa. In Lagos and Ibadan, local printers have been responsible for a flow of novelettes and other literature of an ephemeral nature. In Yoruba this has undoubtedly stimulated local writing of a kind that would not have found its way into print in any other way.

Sound broadcasting was first introduced to Nigeria at the end of the thirties and experiments in using it for educational purposes in schools were undertaken in Lagos immediately. The programmes were completely amateur in production. None of the first participants having had any previous experience in the preparation and production of radio programmes. The initial impact on the schools was negligible. After the end of the Second World War, however, officers from the British Broadcasting Corporation were loaned on secondment to the Nigerian Broadcasting Corporation and an extensive service to schools was developed much along the lines similar to those used in Britain. At the same time selected Nigerians were sent for training to Britain, and the latter have now almost entirely taken over the responsibility for the design and production of the school programmes. Whilst the country is now fully equipped for sound broadcasting, the population coverage is still comparatively small. In the large towns reasonable quality reception is available through rediffusion as well as from direct reception, but for a large part of the country even with the transistor battery operating sets regular reception is not always possible. Even more importantly there is a serious inadequacy as regards maintenance services. This is an aspect of the development of the use of mass media devices for educational purposes that has not received sufficient attention in the past, and still is neglected in much planning of such developments.

Television was first introduced in the Western Region on a commercial basis. In choosing this pattern of service the Government was apparently adopting a system which could be initiated at the minimum cost in terms of capital outlay and which would largely pay for itself. At the same time, the Government hoped to make considerable use of the medium for educational purposes both in the formal education and for the general public. The difficulties of maintaining a satisfactory supply of suitable programme material were not appreciated, and within two years the Western Region Government found itself at odds with its commercial partners over the programmes provided. From the experience gained even in a short time in the Western Region it is clear that the development of television as an effective educational medium will require much experiment on a scale that is beyond the immediate resources of the country, having regard to the urgent needs in other fields of educational endeavour. The technical problems referred to concerning maintenance services of sound broadcasting apply to an even greater extent in the case of television.

A much older, and more fundamental ancillary service is one which has been least satisfactorily developed up to the present

time, that of library facilities. The Commission reporting on the
conditions in the Western Region schools and training colleges
in 1961 remarked:

> It seemed to us that only lip service had been paid to the provision of
> school libraries. Some of the secondary schools and training colleges
> feature small collections, but only a few of them had anything that looked
> like a library, either in collection or accommodation. The primary schools
> not only were without libraries, but were remarkable for their bareness
> and the general absence of any class-room book collection or teaching
> apparatus.*

This state of affairs is not compensated for by the existence of a
library service of a more general character nor is there any
provision in the development plan for the period 1962–8 for
library facilities in schools and colleges.

In the Eastern Region, a library service has been initiated with
a Regional Library at Enugu and a divisional library at Port
Harcourt. In the next phase of development, provision has been
made for the establishment of a children's library at Enugu, and
the building of branch libraries in six divisional towns. In
addition, plans are being devised to expand the skeleton mobile
library service through the use of vans and launches.

The need for library facilities was recognized by the Eastern
Region Government and given effect in 1955 when the Eastern
Nigeria Library Board was brought into being as a result of an
Eastern Nigeria Act which stated: "It shall be the duty of the
Board to take all such steps as may be necessary to establish,
equip, manage and maintain libraries in the Eastern Region."
An agreement was entered into between UNESCO and the
Eastern Region Government in accordance with which UNESCO
undertook to inaugurate a public library service in the region,
and to establish a public library in Enugu. The library service is
free. By 1961 two mobile vans were in service. The library held

* *Report of the Commission appointed to Review the Educational System of Western
Nigeria* (Government Printer, Ibadan, 1961). In Appendix VII there is set
out both commentary and recommendations for meeting the library needs of
the schools and training colleges, and reference is made to the need to link a
school library service with a good library service.

a stock of 32,649 books, kept 7 daily and 5 weekly newspapers, 141 periodicals for adults and 7 periodicals for children. In the year 1960–1, 66,655 books were borrowed by adults, and 25,820 by juveniles from the library in Enugu. In addition through the mobile unit, there were 15,587 adult borrowings and 9603 juvenile borrowings. In a recent evaluation of the project* it was discovered that 21 per cent of the African borrowers regularly read aloud to members of their family or friends. It was also discovered that 40 per cent of the borrowers loaned books to other people. A striking feature of the service is the extent to which the library itself is used as a place for reading. About one-third of the people who enter the library to read or browse are non-members, and of a sample of the members questioned 55 per cent read at the library. The general impression gained from the present use being made of the library is that of its being an adjunct to the formal education system. Books are read as tools for study rather than as an important leisure-time activity. This reflects the intense desire for education and the importance of the practical benefits to be gained. As a pilot project the experience gained should prove of the greatest value to the development and extension of library services in Nigeria and elsewhere, and has clearly demonstrated the importance of an adequate library service at the present stage of the development of formal education system even if the general cultural value is yet to be established. The situation in Northern Nigeria was summarized in a report in† 1963 by Mr. F. A. Sharr. For ten years the Government has been trying to stimulate the growth of a public library system, but despite clear evidence of the potential demand the efforts made had not met with success.

The Regional Library was set up to subsidize the Native Authorities in the provision of libraries, but increasingly its major effort has been directed towards providing a direct service

* S. H. Horrocks, *The Regional Central Library at Enugu, 1961: An Assessment* (UNESCO, Paris, 1962).

† F. A. Sharr, *The Library Needs of Northern Nigeria* (Ministry of Information, Kaduna, 1963), p. 12.

in Kaduna. The reasons given for this are: "a growing realisation that the money and effort put into work with the Native Authorities was not producing results, and the growing pressure of demand from people on the spot in Kaduna, for a variety of reasons, including vacillation of policy, lack of senior staff, and inadequate organisation (for which the library staff is not wholly responsible) the Regional Library is losing momentum and becoming bogged down." The Native Authority Reading Rooms were originally started as public information centres. The policy followed has been to develop them into independent public libraries. But book selection, cataloguing, classification and general organization have been left in the hands of local people, "many of whom are unable to read, and some even to speak English—the language of the books they are supposed to select and organise—and almost none of whom have received any but the most rudimentary training in courses organised at Kaduna". *A Manual for Reading Rooms* had been prepared some years ago for the guidance of the persons put in charge of the reading rooms. In the Report it is recorded: "About a year ago the Regional Library formed the conclusion that this manual needed to be translated into Hausa if the reading room attendants were to understand it; yet its purpose is to teach them how to select, accession, catalogue and classify books in English." As the author of the Report points out, "This contradiction amply illustrates one of the root causes of failure of the present policy."

A policy is proposed which whilst recognizing that the attempt to turn the Native Authority Reading Rooms into public libraries had failed and should be abandoned, advocates clarification of the function of the reading rooms as an active adjunct to public enlightenment and the establishing of new public libraries to serve the reading needs of those who have received education to Primary VI or higher levels. Detailed suggestions are made about the organization of local libraries linked with but not part of a centrally organized regional service. In this respect the proposals differ completely from the policy successfully pursued in Ghana and assume a capacity, at local community levels to organize and support a specialist service, for which there is little evidence of its existence. The question arises whether the author of the report has sufficiently appreciated the nature of the local authorities and the suspicion is aroused that apparent parallelism between the pattern of Northern Nigeria local authorities and local government patterns elsewhere, with which the author of the report is familiar, has resulted in proposals of adoption rather than of adaptation. This is one of the limitations that is likely to occur where advice is based upon limited local knowledge and the adviser is familiar with a system that has been eminently successful in circumstances with which he is so familiar that he fails to appreciate that the success reflects appropriateness of the system to the peculiar conditions of the community.

The need for adequate library facilities both for formal education services and general readership has been clearly stated in the three regions, a pilot project of real value is already being developed in the Eastern Region, the Northern Region has been provided with a guide to policy and a budgeted programme within the capacity of the region's finances, the Western Region has yet to enunciate an overall policy and give expression to it through a properly budgeted programme.

An odd commentary on this state of affairs is provided by the existence of a library school attached to the University at Ibadan. It does not appear to have been thought incongruous to start an expensive project of librarianship training at the University whilst the demand for trained librarians is almost negligible and only very modest provision in relation to needs has been made in two of the regions for library development.

The ancillary service that links with a library service is a museum service and exhibitions. In this respect Nigeria has made a modest but important start. This was begun in Lagos during the war with a temporary exhibition hall. After the end of the war steps were taken to bring into being a National Museum Service and small museums were built at Lagos, Jos and Ife. In 1954, Dr. Kenneth Dike* produced a report for the Government

* See note on following page.

on the care of the archives of the country, and under the direction of Mr. Bernard Fagg a vigorous policy has been pursued for the collection, care and exhibition of artifacts and other materials relevant to the history and knowledge of the country has been vigorously pursued. Some schools are already making use of the resources already available, and there is every reason to believe that with the strong sense of "Nigerian personality" which has developed since independence this aspect of education will show steady growth.

It is worth noting in this respect that the first exhibition of Nigerian Antiquities opened for a period of four weeks in December 1946 attracted 30,000 visitors. In a report made by the Nigeria Public Relations Office at the time, this was "a number which should be an answer to sceptics, who argue that Nigerians are not interested in their own art or history".

Although, as we have noted quite early on, the value of evening classes for adults to supplement their education and to provide them with opportunities of further training had been given limited recognition by the Government providing classes at King's College, Lagos, adult education received no official attention on a significant scale until after 1944. The Christian Churches had brought with them the tradition of the Sunday school system, and in most cases made ability to read the Gospels a qualification for full membership of the Church.

The first major impetus to adult education came from the report of a subcommittee of the Advisory Committee on education in the Colonies published in 1943. Published under the title, *Mass Education in African Society*, the report defined the aims of mass education as follows:

(1) The wide extension of schooling for children with the goal of universal schooling within a measureable time.

(2) The spread of literacy among adults, together with a widespread development of literature and libraries.

* K. O. Dike, *Report on the Preservation and Administration of Historical Records and the Establishment of a Public Record Office in Nigeria* (Government Printer, Lagos, 1954).

(3) The planning of mass education of the community itself, involving the active support of the local community from the start.

(4) The effective co-ordination of welfare plans and mass education plans in order that they might form a comprehensive and balanced whole.

In Northern Nigeria the Government made a great effort to put these objectives into effect. Literacy classes were organized, the resources of Gaskiya Corporation were developed and reading rooms were opened in a large number of centres. In the Eastern Region, the emphasis was placed largely upon community development, and literacy was treated as incidental to community development projects. In the Western Region the main effort was given to literacy classes in the towns. This, in fact, was the obvious course to take because the majority of the Yorubas are urban dwellers though most of them are peasant farmers. As in other countries where the concept of mass education was new, the results varied greatly. The reading rooms in the north, for the most part, soon became the receptacles for dust and waste paper, the local caretakers having neither the incentive nor the training to make the places attractive or to give leadership. In the west, classes were well attended in some places and completely ignored in others. The emphasis that had been placed upon volunteers to run the classes at first met with an enthusiastic response, but after a time it diminished. When, in 1961, the Nigerian Association of University Women investigated women's education in Nigeria, it was found that comparatively few women attended classes. In 1959, 6931 women between the ages of 15 and 50 years enrolled in classes run from July to December. Of those, 4392 completed the courses; 3519 took the test at the end of the course of whom 2673 were awarded certificates. In 1959 the figures were slightly higher; 7595 enrolled; 5259 completed courses; 4383 took the test and 3416 were awarded certificates. The comparable figures for men in 1958 were: enrolled 18,756; completed the course 12,743; sat test 11,784; awarded certificates 9416. In 1959 the enrolment was 14,778; the number completing the course 10,537; candidates for certificates 9662, and the number who obtained certificates was 7375.*

Whilst there can be no doubt about the value of some thousands of adults attaining a modicum of literacy, this scale of participation and success suggests a need to study the motivation or its absence in a community which has a high rate of illiteracy yet is anxious to make rapid social and economic progress.

The first attempts to provide adult education in Nigeria along the lines developed in Britain took place in the years 1947, 1948 and 1949, when tutors from the Oxford University Delegacy for Extra-mural Studies established experimental classes in a number of centres. In 1949 Mr. Robert Gardiner, a Ghanaian, was appointed Director of Extra-mural Studies at the University College, Ibadan. He saw the function of the Department as that of making available adult education facilities for literate men and women who were prepared to undertake serious study for relatively prolonged periods, and also to assist illiterate and semi-literate men and women who showed a real desire to better themselves. He organized three types of activity in addition to the normal sessional courses. These consisted of vacation courses for special groups, radio programmes and a film service. The object of the latter two activities was to arouse interest among the large numbers of people who could not take advantage of the normal extra-mural courses. In an annual report Mr. Gardiner remarked that "In a country where it is estimated that less than 5 per cent of the population is literate the film may prove a very powerful medium for bringing the outside world and modern developments into the experience of the people". He also expressed the opinion that films had something of value to give to the literate part of the population which had not developed a strong habit of reading.

The educational use of film was developed in secondary schools, training colleges, clubs, rural audiences and with some extra-mural groups. In 1951 the Carnegie Corporation gave a grant to

* The Nigerian Association of University Women, *Survey of Women's Education in Nigeria* (Ibadan, 1963).

support the appointment of a visual aids organizer who, in addition to taking responsibility for the National Film Library, built up a library of film-strips in the college, made film-strips embodying local material and also spent much time devising simple and cheap projection apparatus for use by teachers in schools and in training colleges. Though much useful work was done, the concept of a comprehensive service for the whole country was far beyond the resources available to the extra-mural department.

The radio programmes under the title *The Voice of the University College* were intended to make it possible to inform the public of the functions and activities of the College. They were arranged in co-operation with the Radio Division of the Nigeria Public Relations Department during the academic year 1949–50. In 1950 the organization of broadcasting in Nigeria underwent changes and the College programme was discontinued. Although the extra-mural department organized a number of listening groups, they found themselves limited to using the General Overseas Programme of the BBC to provide them with material for discussion until 1955 when Mr. Ogunsheye, then Acting Director of the Department, in co-operation with the Nigerian Broadcasting Service, produced a series of talks for the NBC on the economic development of Nigeria.

The courses organized on a residential basis were closely geared to immediate interests of the people, including courses for professionals and laymen concerned with local government, with the subject of labour management and trade union studies, with journalism, economic development and West African culture.

But the main effort of the Department in terms of money and manpower was put into regular classes dealing with such subjects as English language and literature, French, Latin, economics, political science, history and geography, logic and mathematics, biology and chemistry. Most of the work initially was done in the Western Region, but some classes were organized in the Eastern Region. The governing factor in the development of the Department was shortage of money and the consequent lack of staff. As

money was made available and staff built up the response of
the public grew. In 1954, at a conference of full-time tutors, the
work and policy was assessed and it was decided to modify the
policy by concentrating the services of the full-time tutors on
teaching four or five sessional classes, meeting weekly during the
first two academic terms, and during the third academic term
giving their time to development work and less formal activities
such as one-day schools and week-end conferences.

Professor S. G. Raybould, who spent a period in 1954–5 as
acting Director of the Department, made an assessment of the
situation which still has considerable relevance.

> The situation in which the Department was established was one where
> many kinds of adult education were needed and few agencies exist to supply
> them. There was no lack of opportunity for a university extra-mural
> department to attempt all the tasks proposed for such departments by the
> several reports on higher education in the colonies; to the new college
> and its work widely known throughout the country; to provide oppor-
> tunities for extra-mural study for adults who had not had the chance of a
> full-time university course; to promote education on problems of self-
> government; to organise "refresher" courses for professional workers and
> similar students; to influence other forms of adult education; and by
> these means to bring members of the college into association with Nigerians
> of all kinds and in all regions.*

The attempt to make some contribution along all these lines
ended in 1955 when it was decided to concentrate attention upon
those aspects of adult education normally associated in the British
tradition with a university. In addition, it was decided to confine
the classes to a limited number of centres instead of attempting
countrywide coverage.

With the establishment of additional universities at Nsukka
in the east, Zaria in the north, and the additional universities
of Ife and Lagos in the west, the time has come for another
reassessment of the functions of extra-mural departments in
Nigerian education.

One of the ancillary education services that is most in demand
is that of providing machinery whereby educational attainment

* S. G. Raybould, *Adult Education at a Tropical University* (Longmans, London,
1957), p. 44.

can be assessed and candidates selected for further training or employment. Little attention was given to the provision of public examinations in Nigeria until 1950, though from the very early days the secondary schools had made use of the examination facilities provided by the Cambridge Schools Examinations Syndicate, teachers seeking some form of special professional recognition had taken the examinations of the College of Preceptors in London, and individuals hoping to obtain opportunities for advanced education had made use of the University of London Matriculation examination. Official action was limited to organizing local examinations for the training colleges and for the award primary school leaving certificate. (Government departments for the purposes of recruitment organized competitive examinations under their own auspices.) It was not considered that the duties called for any special knowledge or skill or experience. A person might be called upon to set examination questions and mark the papers one year and never be concerned with such work again. The task of organizing the examinations was regarded as a normal part of the duties of education officers and staffs of schools and colleges. Such an amateur approach might have been permissible when numbers were small and a great deal could be settled by personal contacts, but it was an approach that could not be maintained as the numbers grew rapidly in the 1940's.

It was not until 1950, when Dr. G. B. Jeffery, Director of the London Institute of Education, was invited by the Secretary of State for the Colonies to visit West Africa and to report upon a proposal that there should be instituted a West African Schools Examination Council that the matter was again considered.* A proposal made by E. R. Swanston in 1927–8 that a local schools examination organization should be set up in order that the examination requirements might be more closely related to

† G. B. Jeffery, *Report to the Secretary of State for the Colonies on a Visit to West Africa* (Government Printing Dept., Accra, 1950). The West Africa Examinations Council produces a report annually which provides detailed information about the work.

local needs, failed to get the approval of the Board of Education which was dominated by local African influence. Apart from the considerations already referred to, Dr. Jeffery was faced with the contention that the examination system had produced a disgruntled, agitating type of individual possessing paper qualifications and nothing else. This view can only be described as a jaundiced one; but it was true that the overwhelming anxiety of most candidates to pass their examinations resulted in slavish attention to the details of the syllabus which undoubtedly narrowed the general value of the studies of many pupils.

As a result of his investigations Dr. Jeffery came to the conclusion ". . . not that examinations should be abolished or discouraged . . . but that the questions of what examinations should be made available and the way in which they can best be adapted to educational purposes are of the very greatest educational importance, and should be decided on educational grounds alone by the best available West Africa educational opinion and experience". In his report he distinguished between three types of examination. There was the "external examination" which prescribed a scheme and set a standard for the individual student working in isolation. There was the "school examination" which assumed the co-operation of the teacher with the university examining body and which assumed that the teacher was able and willing to exercise professional responsibility for keeping a balance between educational activity and examination needs. Thirdly, there was the "competitive examination" used for the award of scholarships or appointments. At the time that he was reporting, the University of London was mainly responsible for providing examinations of the first category. The Cambridge Schools Examinations Syndicate had made commendable efforts to meet local needs whilst maintaining parity of standards in relation to English requirements for the second category of examinations. Of the third category of examination, Dr. Jeffery found that there was urgent need to establish a system for competitive and selection examinations specific to West Africa.

After his report was accepted by the British and the West

African governments, a Council was established composed of representatives of the Nigerian, Gold Coast, Sierra Leone and Gambian governments, a number of teachers, representatives of the university colleges of Ibadan, Gold Coast and Fourah Bay, and representatives of the University of London and of the Cambridge Schools Examinations Syndicate. The latter had agreed to continue to run examinations for the secondary schools but with the understanding that over a period of years the co-operation between the West Africa Examinations Council and the Syndicate would be changed until the former became entirely responsible for school examinations in West Africa.

The first examinations organized entirely by the West Africa Examinations Council were civil service promotion examinations for the Gold Coast Government. Unfortunately, the very first exercise was marked by a serious defect that has continued to be a source of anxiety and embarrassment, namely leakage of the question papers. Despite this setback the Council pressed forward with its work. During the first ten years, despite the generosity of the governments and the extensive consultation and discussion of plans, the Council found itself continually pressed to undertake more work than it was able to undertake.

The first attempt to take over responsibility for setting and marking the English Language paper in the School Certificate Examination brought out a difficulty which still exists, that of providing an adequate supply of local examiners to carry out the marking to schedule. Although ample thought had been given to this problem before it was decided to undertake the experiment, between the time that elapsed in the setting of the paper and the appointing of the examiners, and the taking of the paper by the candidates, there were severe losses of examiners through sickness, transfer of appointment and other reasons. Fortunately, the resources of the Cambridge Syndicate were in reserve. But the experience served to underline the fact that it was a very different matter trying to find examiners in a situation where the number of examinees was increasing exceedingly rapidly and there was a shortage of practising teachers and virtually no pool of retired teachers to draw upon as examiners.

One task that the Council had to undertake which by its numerical size created a problem was that of providing a school-leaving examination for the Gold Coast middle schools. The Ministry of Education had come to the conclusion that with the changes in the level of qualifications for admission to certain types of work, the Middle School Leaving Certificate was no longer necessary. This coupled with the anticipated rate of growth of the middle schools suggested that dropping the examination was sound on both educational and economic grounds. Within two years public pressure forced the Ministry to reinstate the examination. During the two years the expansion of the middle schools had been such that an examination along the old lines was quite impossible to organize. As a result, a new examination along objective test lines was designed and organized on an *ad hoc* basis by the Institute of Education of the University College of the Gold Coast, and a year later this was taken over by the West Africa Examinations Council which introduced machine marking to deal with the numbers involved.

The large numbers of private candidates in Nigeria who made use of the University of London General Certificate of Education presented another problem. Apart from the organizational problems of providing the examination in centres spread throughout the country, an unduly high proportion of the candidates were so inadequately prepared for the examination that there was a large failure rate. This meant not only much fruitless work on the part of administrators and the examiners but also wasted expenditure of relatively large sums of money by candidates who could not afford it. To cope with this problem, the Council introduced a special qualifying examination which weeded out the obvious failures at much less cost and at the same time saved the weak candidates from wasting their money.

The Council, however, did not confine itself merely to the task of organizing and running examinations. Following the experience and advice of the Cambridge Syndicate, the Council set up subject panels whose membership was drawn from the teachers in the secondary schools and from the university colleges to review the subject syllabuses. One of the outcomes of this step was the adoption of alternative syllabuses in history to provide for schools where the study of the history of the impact of Islam was more relevant in some respects than the study of aspects of British history. Similarly, an alternative religious knowledge paper based upon Moslem studies was provided for the Moslem schools in Northern Nigeria. The Council also gave attention to the problem of recognizing African languages for inclusion in the School Certificate Examination, and experimented with the design and use of an oral English examination in co-operation with the Phonetics Department of the University College of the Gold Coast. The difficulties of the English Language paper were given serious attention from the beginning, and the study of them was made the subject of a special report submitted to the Council. In order to counteract the shortage of experienced examiners, in 1962 the Council organized at the University College, Ibadan, a special course on examination problems and procedures.

Despite the difficulties and the setbacks, the Council has provided a service which has already proved of great value to Nigeria and to the countries with which its service is shared. Its work is none the easier to perform because it has to satisfy the interests of four national and three regional governments. The geographical extent of its responsibilities already involve three separate offices, and the growth in number of universities, whilst offering the advantage of a greater number of university teachers from which to recruit examiners and consultants, also provides the possibilities of complications in syllabus requirements.

In addition to the examination requirements met by the facilities offered through the West African Examinations Council, trade and industry and government departments have found it necessary to obtain specialist assistance in selecting trainees where skills other than those measured by written examinations are of importance. The first indications of this need appeared in 1951 when the West African Command decided that it had to improve its methods of selection of soldiers recruited for trade training. Fortunately, Mr. Andrew Taylor, then a senior lecturer in psychology in the University College of the Gold Coast Institute of Education, was available for consultation and was able to devise a pilot project* based upon the experience of Dr. S. Biesheuvel in the South African mining industry. This marked the beginning of a programme which included service to the mining industry, trading firms, the police, the Health Department and Ghana Airways, and eventually the establishment of a self-contained unit which was taken over by the Ghana Government. This development in Ghana was extended to Nigeria when Shell–BP began the construction of the oil wells in the Niger delta and required a similar service in selecting local recruits for training for the new industry. The need for such selection services will grow rapidly as the pace of industrialization quickens. Whilst the University of Ibadan through the Institute of Education will doubtless be able to give some assistance in these developments, the establishment of an organization specializing in the design and application of suitable selection procedures appears to be inevitable.

The West African Examinations Council has already undertaken the setting up of an Aptitude Testing Board and Unit in Nigeria, and expects by 1966 to have introduced a measure of objective testing in the school certificate examinations. These developments are a direct consequence of bringing to bear upon West Africa examination problems experience built up elsewhere, and particularly in the United States.†

It was natural that in a British colony the possibilities of such movements as the Boy Scouts, Girl Guides, Boys Brigade and the like should be exploited for their special contribution to training in citizenship. During the 1930's and 1940's branches of these movements were started in Nigeria with support from

* A. Taylor, *Personnel Selection, West African Command Pilot investigation* (UCGC, Accra, 1954). A. Taylor (Ed.), *Educational and Occupational Selection in West Africa* (Oxford University Press, London, 1962).

† West African Schools Examinations, *The Times Educational Supplement* (London), 8 May 1964, p. 1244.

Government and the missions. Despite the efforts made, which in the case of the Scout Movement included the establishment of a training camp, the results were not at all impressive. Some critics referred to the members as "Empire Day Scouts" because of the way in which they were in the public eye at Empire Day parades and celebrations. Reflection on the activities and organization suggests that the comparative failure was due to two main causes. In the first place these movements were almost entirely extra-curricular activities of the better equipped and staffed schools. Secondly, there was virtually no adaptation of the activities to local conditions. They were, in fact, examples of activities developed in one country to meet a particular set of problems and then transferred, on the assumption that the same problems existed in the same circumstances in another country. The experience suggests that the satisfactory provision of organized activities for Nigerian adolescents has yet to be devised, and that the devising of suitable schemes will call for more imagination and understanding of local interests and needs than has been shown hitherto. Where it is decided to transfer organizations and services the burden of proof that the transfer will be effective is a heavy one. Too often the reasoning behind a proposal is because a particular organization exists in a more advanced country it should be re-created in a less advanced country. In fact, many ancillary education features in highly industrialized countries exist because some feature of the industrial society makes them necessary or, because, though unimportant they can be afforded. Their transfer to an underdeveloped country can be disastrous, and if not disastrous harmful in that they draw resources and energies from the tasks that are vital for development. To suggest that the organizations here referred to might have been harmful rather than beneficial to Nigeria may offend some people. But good intentions are no excuse for continuing in error. Failure and indifferent success should stimulate efforts to understand more fully the complexity of the task of education and is particularly necessary in respect of ancillary activities which are often dependent upon the enthusiasm of dedicated people whose zeal is the justification for the drive put into the particular service.

The provision of ancillary services is an important part of any programme of educational development, but it is a part that calls for a tough appreciation of the relative importance of the ancillary activities relative to the main strategic needs. A comment made in another context by Mr. J. K. Galbraith might well serve to underline this point:

> A hundred years ago the development of the trans-Mississippi plains in the United States called above all else for a land policy which would get the land settled and plowed and a transportation system which would get the products to market. To this end the government surveyed the land, gave 160 acres to anyone who had proved his good intentions by farming it for a few months, and subsidized the building of railways. These essentials being provided, development proceeded with unexampled speed. It was our unquestioned good fortune that community education experts, grain marketing analysts, home advisers, vocational counselors, communication specialists or public safety counselors had not been invented. Had these existed, attention would have been drawn from the strategically central task of getting the farms settled and the railways built. And they would have been a burden on the backs of people who could ill afford such luxuries.*

The importance of this comment lies in the fact that Nigeria, like other countries, offers many openings to outside agencies who wish to offer aid, especially in the area of ancillary educational activities. For the intending donor the attractions are great, because they offer opportunities for spectacular display of good works which attract attention because they bring something new to the recipient country and generally make an appeal to the interested parties in the donor country. This is a part of the wider question of external aid generally to which more detailed attention will be given later.

The provision of textbooks as an ancillary service grew up in response to the local needs. For the missionary-controlled schools, the supply of textbooks was dealt with through a group of missionary bookshops. The CMS Bookshop organization started as the individual effort of the Mission Secretary, using a

---

* J. K. Galbraith, *Economic Development in Perspective* (Harvard University Press. Oxford University Press, London, 1962), p. 27.

table in his office. The success of this effort eventually led to the establishment of a Bookshop organization which represented the major means of supplying books for schools until the thirties of this century. Other mission organizations developed their own bookshops. Government schools were catered for through the purchasing machinery of the Crown Agents for the Colonies. No attempt was made to establish special government-controlled machinery either for the provision or distribution of textbooks. In the mission schools the pupils had to buy their own textbooks. In government schools, textbooks were treated as part of the school equipment.

The actual production of textbooks was left almost entirely to the commercial publishers in the United Kingdom except for isolated efforts at local production by the mission presses and a few special items printed by the Government Press and, latterly, for Northern Nigeria, the publishing of textbooks, particularly in Hausa, for use in the Northern Nigeria schools.

With the rapid expansion of education, the capacity of the mission bookshops to provide an adequate service was strained to the limit. Some of the United Kingdom publishers, who had previously handled all their sales through the mission bookshops, both wholesale and retail, set up local warehouse facilities and appointed local representatives and sales managers to cope better with the increasing demands. With independence governments took a greater interest in the problem. In the Western Region the bulk ordering of books for direct distribution to the schools was attempted, but the initial efforts ran into difficulties, mainly because of the inexactness of the information necessary, but also because the education service was not well enough equipped to deal with the problem. The Native Authorities now put out the textbook requirements to tender.

Government interest in the local production of textbooks has grown out of concern for the costs of the supply of textbooks and out of concern for developing local authorship and more direct control over the contents of the books. Nigeria took immediate advantage of the provision of a course in the design, production and distribution of textbooks at the University of London Institute of Education following decisions taken at the Commonwealth Education Conference held at Delhi in 1962 to train officers for appointments in the ministries. In addition, more recently, encouragement has been given to the Franklin Book Programs Inc., an American Foundation whose function is to assist printing, publication and distribution of books in any way they can that is compatible with local needs and established local relationships. This Foundation has been established in the conviction that "a healthy and creative indigenous book industry is basic to educational and economic advance". The introduction of the English Language Book Society series of cheap university textbooks in 1963, an extension of a cheap-books scheme first sponsored by the United Kingdom Government in India and Pakistan, proved most opportune because it helped to offset the reductions in grants to students introduced by Government to ease the burden on government funds.

Whilst in the early days the local distribution of books generally presented great difficulty, and this is still held to be a matter of some seriousness, a recent survey of the situation suggested that this is no longer so, and that the problem is now essentially one of books being available in the market, and the congestion that arises during the short period at the beginning of the school year. This latter problem arises because more than 95 per cent of all book sales in Nigeria are educational; and 90 per cent of those sales take place between the end of December and the beginning of February. The bulk of the rest of the sales are university books, and they have their "season" in October. For both seasons difficulties occur because of the failure of the appropriate persons to prescribe the books early enough for orders to be placed to ensure that they can be delivered on time.

The significance of this service cannot be overestimated. In economic terms it represents at the present time a sum of approximately £1,500,000 per annum. This is a figure that is likely to double during the next decade, assuming that growth is related to the increase in numbers of pupils alone. If all the pupils and students were to be provided with all the books they are expected to have the increase would be very much greater in value. Whether this service remains in the hands of private enterprise or becomes largely the responsibility of official agencies the need to make it an efficient service is of paramount import both educationally and financially.

CHAPTER 7

THE UNIVERSITIES
AND TEACHER EDUCATION

IN THEIR report published in 1945 the Commission on Higher
Education in West Africa found it necessary to give a chapter to
the subject of the supply and training of teachers.* The reasons
they offered for their action were, firstly, the existence of teacher-
training courses in the centres of higher education at Fourah Bay
College in Sierra Leone, at Achimota in the Gold Coast and at
Yaba Higher College in Nigeria; secondly, because the recruits
for higher education come from the secondary schools the
standards and the qualification of the staffs of the secondary
schools were matters of concern in planning a policy for higher
education.

The position they found was that a small number of the
Africans on the staffs of the secondary schools had taken degrees
and diplomas of education in Britain, a greater number had taken
degrees and diplomas of education at Fourah Bay College and
the great majority of the African secondary school teachers,
however, were non-graduates, mostly possessing the highest
grade of teachers' certificate available in the country. Those who
were graduates had, of course, followed normal degree courses
developed in Britain. Even at Fourah Bay College, which was
affiliated to Durham University, the syllabuses followed were
exactly the same as those studied in the latter institution. No
attempt was made to relate the subject-matter to the local
environment. This was also true of the courses leading to the
examinations for the diploma in education with the exception of

* *Report of the Commission on Higher Education in West Africa* (Cmd. 6655, HMSO,
London, 1945), ch. 5,

the courses that had been devised in the Colonial Department of the University of London Institute of Education. However, the number of Nigerians who had obtained professional training in London was at that time so small as to have little or no impact upon the work in the Nigerian secondary schools.

The Commission recognized that the way the teachers were educated and trained contributed to the narrow academic nature of the work done in secondary schools, and suggested that three steps should be taken to remedy the situation.

Their first recommendation was that all the non-graduate staff in the secondary schools should have an opportunity of wider academic study under university conditions. They suggested that this might be done in the proposed new university colleges by admitting a small number of teachers to attend appropriate courses for one year as members of regular classes; the purpose being to widen the cultural outlook and to increase the intellectual interest of the teachers in the subjects they taught. Secondly, they suggested that as soon as it was possible to do so, new recruits to the staffs of the secondary schools should have passed through an intermediate course at one of the university colleges and received, in addition, two years of professional training. This proposal, they recognized as an interim measure because the need for a great increase in the number of secondary-school teachers was so urgent, that for some time to come there was no prospect of an adequate supply of graduates.

Their third recommendation was made on account of the gulf they found between modern thought on secondary education in Britain and elsewhere and in West Africa. They expressed the view that the men and women, of whatever race, who held posts of special responsibility in the secondary schools "should be aware of the ferment in educational ideas and methods which is characteristic of the western world at the present time, and should be aware too of the changing needs and new emphases in African education. To achieve this meeting place of Western and African thought will be one of the tasks of the Institute of Education for West Africa." As an interim measure they suggested that where possible, heads of secondary schools and leading members of staffs should be given the opportunity of attending refresher courses in Great Britain in order to observe and discuss new ideas and methods with men and women from other countries.

In their concern about the narrow academic nature of the secondary school curriculum, the Commission made a number of observations on the training of secondary-school teachers. In their view it was essential that the teacher-training course should be professional in character and should not be mixed up with the general education of the intending teacher. They were of the opinion that following a good general secondary education there should be at least two years of academic work in a university institution where the students would learn how to study independently, handle reference material, apparatus and equipment, and that this should be followed by two years of professional training, "when they learn by observation and by practice in teaching, to adapt their new-found knowledge to children of different age levels, to understand, again by observation as well as by reading, the mental, physical and moral development of children, and to see, by studying the community and its needs, the process of education as something much wider than giving lessons in a classroom or a laboratory". They made the further observation that as the teacher is an important and responsible servant to the community, he should by observation and by formal instruction learn about the nature and needs of his own society.

The first steps to follow-up these recommendations were taken, not in Nigeria, but in London. One member of the Commission, Dr. Margaret Read, was in charge of the Colonial Department of the University of London Institute of Education. With the support of the Director, Sir Fred Clarke and the encouragement of the Colonial Office, she anticipated the publication and acceptance of the Report by starting a course for experienced non-graduates. Among the first students were three Mallams from Northern Nigeria, including the head of a secondary school who later was to become the Federal Prime Minister of Nigeria, Alhaji Sir Abubakar Tafewa Balewa.

The suggestion that there should be an Institute of Education to serve West Africa was accepted by all concerned with the implementation of the Report, and on the assumption that in the early stages of university development it should be a part of the University College of the Gold Coast, serving Gambia, Sierre Leone, the Gold Coast and Nigeria—the setting-up of an institute or department in Nigeria was not given immediate priority in the programme for University College Ibadan. This proved to be an unfortunate decision. Because the governments and the colleges were unable to arrive at a satisfactory solution to the problem of sharing the costs of the department, which was intended to provide a common service, few Nigerian students were able to make use of the facilities provided at the University College of the Gold Coast. For the same reason the Gold Coast was unable to take advantage of the Medical School established at Ibadan. A start, however, was made at the Zaria branch of the Nigerian College of Arts Science and Technology, where an education department was organized to provide special courses for experienced non-graduate teachers to qualify either as junior secondary school teachers or as training college tutors. It was not until 1956 that the University College, Ibadan, took steps to establish a Department and Institute of Education.

In the first instance, the Institute provided two professional courses of training—a post-graduate certificate in education of one academic year in length under the scheme of special relationship with the University of London, and a one-year course for trained experienced non-graduates. The latter course was not related to the special relationship scheme, but closely resembled the course provided at the University College of the Gold Coast, which in its turn was derived from the course already referred to, organized in London in 1944. In addition to providing these courses, short courses were organized for teachers in service, and steps were taken to inaugurate research into certain aspects of child development, selection methods, and curricular studies. With the establishment of the University of Nigeria, Nsukka, a second college of education came into being, and in 1962 the Department of Education of the Nigerian College of Arts Science and Technology at Zaria was made part of the Ahmadu Bello University. A further addition at the university level of facilities for the training of teachers was proposed by the UNESCO Commission in 1961 in their recommendations for the establishment of the University of Lagos.*

The proposals made for the Faculty of Education in the University of Lagos suggested that in addition to a one-year post-graduate diploma course, there should also be provided a three-year undergraduate course leading to a bachelor's degree and a teacher's diploma. This latter idea was one which had been discussed at meetings of the heads of the departments and institutes of education in English-speaking Africa, at a conference held at the University College, Makevere, Uganda, in 1961. This idea was generally accepted, and in 1962 was adopted at the University of Ibadan as an additional way of contributing to the demand for trained graduate teachers. This represented a break with the British tradition of considerable importance. In the first place, two academic subjects were to be studied to degree level, whereas the English universities had been moving increasingly towards intensive specialization of honours schools in one subject. Secondly, the study of education was placed within the academic context whilst maintaining its professional status. By requiring practical work in education to be carried out during vacation terms, and incorporating the theoretical studies of education in the degree structure, the supply of secondary school teachers can be considerably increased.

Whilst the universities in Nigeria have thus responded to a requirement expressed in turn by the Elliot, Ashby and the UNESCO Commissions to make provision for the training of teachers for the secondary schools, one objective set forth in different ways by the various commissions has not been achieved, namely that of promoting closer co-operation and co-ordination

* *The Establishment of the University of Lagos* (UNESCO, Paris, 1961).

between the university departments of education and other teacher-training centres.

It is worth noting that the concept of all teacher-training coming under the aegis of the universities is one that has been pursued in Britain for over twenty years. Yet there is still much to be done as is clearly indicated in the Robbins Report* on Higher Education published in 1963. In Nigeria, apart from the fact that the universities are of so recent origin, they have to cater for a population spread over a much larger country lacking the means of communication to be found in Britain.

In Northern Nigeria steps were taken to co-ordinate the work of the training colleges with that of the Education Department of the Nigeria College at Zaria. It had been assumed that the Institute of Education at Ibadan would have acted in some fashion for the whole country, but the number of training colleges envolved, the distances to be covered, and the small number of staff available precluded any possibility of developing any scheme similar to those that had been devised in Britain. The establishment of a number of advanced training colleges has provided potential centres through which the universities might work, but it appears almost inevitable that for some time to come the universities will be unable to follow the direction taken in this respect in Britain. In these circumstances, it is probable that the influence of the institutes of education will be exerted more through the development of regular workshops and conferences for key groups, such as heads of schools, training college tutors, and through the dissemination of the results of such activities in publications such as the *West African Journal of Education.*† This is edited by members of the Ibadan Institute of Education with the assistance of an editorial board representative of all the departments and institutes of education as well as of the ministries of education in Nigeria.

In addition to the special contribution that the universities

---

* Committee on Higher Education, *Higher Education: Report of the Committee under the Chairmanship of Lord Robbins* (HMSO, London, 1963).
† *West African Journal of Education*, Ibadan University Institute of Education.

have to make through institutes and departments of education, providing courses of training, facilities for research into education, in-service training, conferences and workshops, the universities have another contribution to make, and that is in the field of curriculum and African studies.

The need to adapt the curriculum to the environment has continually been the subject of comment. Reference has already been made to attempts to carry out suitable adaptations and changes, yet the same criticisms are still made and, for the most part, have considerable validity. One of the more important reasons for this is that the people who have tried to modify the curriculum were working more or less in isolation, but another, and more important reason is the absence of the information on which to base curriculum changes. The source of the necessary knowledge lies in the universities. But the universities of Nigeria are not Nigerian universities; they are British and American universities where Nigerians can take good degrees having international currency without knowing anything about Nigeria. There is nothing remarkable about this state of affairs. It is now clearly recognized that American universities have their own characteristic organization and that their courses are peculiarly American in orientation and in content. But less than 100 years ago, C. W. Eliot, who became President of Harvard, wrote:

> A university, in any worthy sense of the term, must grow from seed. It cannot be transplanted from England or Germany in full leaf and bearing. It cannot be run up, like a cotton mill, in six months, to meet a quick demand. . . . When the American university appears, it will not be a copy of foreign institutions . . . but the slow and natural outgrowth of American social and political habits.*

It was inevitable, in Nigeria as in the United States, that the first objective of the newly established universities was to gain acceptance in the university world. That stage has been reached. The next stage incorporating and codifying the knowledge of the local situation and circumstances into the undergraduate curriculum in the universities and the dissemination of the appropriate knowledge throughout the education system is, in many ways

* C. W. Eliot, The new education, *Atlantic Monthly*, **23**, 1869.

more formidable. Apart from collecting the facts and arranging
them in a disciplined and systematic fashion, they must be presented in a way which will be meaningful to the mass of the
people as well as to the intellectual *élite*. Sir Eric Ashby commenting upon the need for this to be done remarks:

> If universities are to put down roots in tropical Africa the first step must
> surely be to study traditional African societies and the way they change
> under the influence of the West, as a compulsory subject at the core of the
> curriculum; not simply as a somewhat unconventional option. . . . For the
> danger in West Africa is similar to the danger to which India has suc-
> cumbed: that the inevitable gap between the intellectuals and the mass of
> the population will widen until in the end even kinship ties and tribal
> loyalty may be unable to bridge it.*

Dr. S. O. Biobaku expressed similar anxieties from another
angle, namely: "that politicians might exert pressure upon the
universities if the latter failed to respond quickly enough to the
need for the university to take an active part in promoting a new
life and making independence a reality." The awareness of the
need for action was also expressed by those responsible for the
establishment of the University of Nigeria: ". . . such a higher
institution should not only be cultural, according to the classical
concept of universities, but it should also be vocational in its
objective and Nigerian in its content."† Whilst the latter institution sought to realize this objective by following a philosophy
based upon the pattern of the American land grant colleges, the
University of Ibadan and the University of Ife have placed
greater emphasis upon the development of research programmes
of a long-term nature in historical and sociological studies. This
reflects the process of growth referred to by Eliot in that the
inspirers of the programmes in each institution, Dr. Dike at
Ibadan, Dr. Biobaku at the University of Ife and Dr. Azikwe, the
inspirer of the University of Nigeria, each starting from the
backgrounds of their own scholastic careers, seek a common goal,

* Sir Eric Ashby, *Functions of Universities in the West African Intellectual Community*, edited by J. T. Saunders and M. Dowuona (Ibadan University Press,
1962), p. 55.
† Eastern Region of Nigeria, *University of Nigeria: Progress Report* (Government
Printer, Enugu, 1960), p. 3,

namely universities indigenous to the country. It is not without significance that the area of knowledge in which the first fruits of local study have been made available in textbook form is that of geography, as early as 1955, when Buchanan and Pugh produced the textbook *Land and People of Nigeria* based upon studies carried out at the University College of Ibadan.

If, however, this process of growth and localization of the curriculum is to be accelerated, there will have to be much more intensive co-operation between those responsible for research and teaching in the several disciplines in the universities and the people responsible for the work in the schools and in the training colleges. In this respect, of the greatest value is the *active* participation of members of the university teaching staff in the work of the examining bodies and the co-operation of several different groups in curriculum studies and experiments such as the mathematics curriculum study sponsored by Educational Services Incorporated. In this project members of the Mathematics Department and the Institute of Education, members of training college staffs and officials of the Ministry of Education, Western Region, are all participating in the design and testing of material. An important feature of this project is that the participants are as much concerned with the subject at the primary as at the secondary level. A similar project for elementary science has been begun at the University of Nigeria, Nsukka.

Such developments, however, are still somewhat sporadic. Recent revisions of primary school syllabuses in history and arithmetic carried out merely by consultation bear all the marks of the old recipe served up with minor variations, and show little understanding of the needs of the country. Many of the expatriate staff and some of the Nigerian intellectuals are reluctant to recognize that Nigerian culture and organization of society are worth studying by undergraduates. Yet the teacher and the civil servant who share the responsibility for leading Nigeria from the old ways of life to the new ways will not be able to do so unless they possess at least some knowledge of these and other aspects of Nigerian society and the Nigerian environment.

The difficulties in dealing with this problem are reflected in much of the current work on the revision of the syllabuses and the curricula. Examination of a recently revised history syllabus for use in the Eastern Region and comparison with past syllabuses reveals but a superficial adaptation and minor adjustment of content and treatment that shows little awareness of the historical studies that have been carried out in Nigeria and but a superficial understanding of what adaptation really involves. Part of the difficulty lies in the fact that most of the people involved in the work are still ill-equipped for the task. In addition, the pressure to expand the education system and the limitations of the majority of teachers in respect of their own academic knowledge and professional competence make it difficult for the education authorities to press for radical changes in content and methods.

The difficulties created for the universities, and in particular their institutes and departments of education by this problem of relating the content of education to the society, are intensified by the inevitable pressure for accelerating the rate of change. If wise decisions are to be made, there must be time for experiment, evaluation and testing of ideas. In some matters the rate of growth and adaptation are completely dependent upon the productive capacity of the scholars and the amount of time that can be given to research in addition to current teaching duties.

In 1945 the Commission on Higher Education in West Africa stressed the need for research in child development and into language teaching. Significant studies in the former field represent long-term investigations lasting for periods of twelve to fifteen years. Such studies could not be undertaken until competent Nigerian research workers were available. In consequence the training colleges are still largely dependent upon such interpretation tutors can make of generally accepted ideas established in other societies. Similarly, the lack of scholars in the field of linguistics has meant that the provision of materials in Nigerian languages is still dependent upon the good intentions of individuals working in their spare time and with such linguistic equipment as they happen to have picked up.

These are examples of a situation in which the universities are caught on the horns of a dilemma. The needs of the educational system are so great that there is continuing pressure upon the universities to provide immediate answers. If they do so, they are in danger of being accused of superficiality. The scholars themselves are fearful of their reputations. If they do not attempt to produce interim solutions they are likely to be accused of an "ivory-tower" outlook. Up to the present the path pursued has been peculiar to each department and, in some cases, characteristic of particular persons. In part, the answer lies in a more effective exchange of views between the universities and the ministries of education so that a more thorough understanding of problems and their solutions can be arrived at and in part, in more thorough sharing of resources as between universities.

In the newly established National Universities Commission and the All-Nigeria Academic Council, machinery exists to deal with the latter problem, but in respect of the relations between the universities and the ministries of education much depends upon personalities in day-to-day contacts. The difficulties are enhanced where in addition to the University Institute of Education there is an external agency ready and anxious to make some special contribution to a specific educational problem. The agency may be very certain of the validity of the solution it offers and strengthens its case by the generosity of the financial backing it is prepared to give in support of the project. In these circumstances, the civil servants being under constant pressure to expand and improve the educational facilities may be moved to take decisions that the staff of the Institute of Education able to exercise more objective judgement might well question. On the other hand, failure to consult all those who think they ought to be consulted, may result in a project, which has the full support of the university, being frowned upon or directly rejected by the civil servants. Minor clashes of these kinds have taken place. That they have done so, reflects the highly fluid state of affairs consequent upon the newness of the university institutions and the comparative lack of experience of some of the political heads and permanent staff of ministries. In these circumstances the part to be played by the universities in making their contribution to the expansion and the development of the education system is much more delicate and complicated than it is where the universities and institutes of education are already accepted and acceptable parts of the society they exist to serve.

One aspect of the contribution of the universities to general education which is related to the contribution of the universities to teacher education is that of the development of African Studies. Dr. S. Biobaku, Pro Vice-Chancellor of the University of Ife, has recently discussed the problem in what might be described as an apologia for the recently established Institute of African Studies at the University of Ife*. He recognized that in Africa there was until recently "neither the impulse nor the duty to establish the existence and affirm the value of an African culture and assist its transmission to, and diffusion among, its peoples". In pleading the case for African studies he points out that the African universities have to cultivate the study of those subjects which have universal concern and validity and also, by using the techniques of study and research which have universal validity, pursue the study of their own African inheritance and environment. In one outspoken passage he gives a clear warning of the difficulties involved.

> This enterprise is beset with pitfalls. It has its own dangers. First it involves a rediscovery of the true past of Africa and the Africans, but this must not be romanticized unduly; it must not degenerate into chasing a past glory that never existed. There must be no pandering to the African jingoists by simply rejecting one extreme view of regarding Africa as having no worthwhile culture whatsoever and embracing the other, of idealizing everything African. Secondly, the magnitude of the task of reorientation should not be underrated. It must be remembered that the unfolding of a culture which has long been in decay is more than a lifetime assignment for any scholar. It can be accomplished only after prolonged study and research involving several generations of scholars. Thirdly, there is the danger of falsifying findings in order to conform with ephemeral notions of past glories or to suit some transient political necessities. On no account should the scholar compromise his academic integrity or connive at the enthronement of mediocrity just because it pleases.

* S. Biobaku, African studies in an African University, *Minerva* 1 (3) (1963) 287.

The Institute of African Studies set up at the University of Ife to ensure the proper contribution to African Studies has been organized as an interdisciplinary research centre, concentrating initially on post-graduate studies while working towards the establishment of undergraduate teaching. Two types of seminar have been developed; open seminars which anyone may attend on signifying their attention to do so, and staff seminars limited to the staff of the Institute and invited persons having special knowledge and interest in the subject under review.

This is clearly a conservative approach to an area of study and education that many people would regard as of the greatest urgency. But it is an approach which indicates a maturity of outlook that has general support in the country, and is, therefore to be seen as the appropriate answer in the circumstances.

CHAPTER 8

PROBLEMS OF ADAPTATION

IN 1921, in their report *Education in Africa*, the Phelps–Stokes Commission stated: "The adaptation of education to the needs of the individual and the community is increasingly emphasized in the recommendations of American and European educators."[*] Forty-two years later, in the introduction to a report on a comparative education seminar abroad organized for a group of Nigerians, Dr. Adam Skapski remarks: "Their main and most important task was to find out what particular features, observed in the foreign educational systems, might be profitably adapted in Nigeria."[†]

In this chapter, it is proposed to examine four recent *adoptions* from overseas which raise questions of *adaptation*.

In 1951 there was organized at Man O' War Bay, Victoria, Southern (now West) Cameroon, a training centre designed to inculcate in all the participants a spirit of responsible and enlightened citizenship[‡]. The training course was initiated exactly along the lines of the Outward Bound course that had been developed in Britain. It was hoped that through living and working together, sharing the rigours of mountain-climbing, digging roads, building bridges and learning to accept a strict discipline based upon the need for mutual co-operation and shared responsibility the participants, drawn from clerical and administrative work in government, commercial and industrial walks of life, would develop a more enlightened sense of citizenship,

[*] L. J. Lewis (Ed.), *Phelps–Stokes Report on Education in Africa* (abridged, Oxford University Press, 1962), p. 23.
[†] Ministry of Education Eastern Nigeria, *Report of the Comparative Education Seminar* (Official Document No. 24 of 1963), p. 3.
[‡] P. E. N. Malafa, Man O' War Bay assumes a new Role, *Oversea Education*, **34** (4) (1963) 157–61.

understand better the need for unity and respect for honest leadership.

Two features of life in Nigeria were given special attention. In the first place, it was recognized that the concept of being members of one nation could not become a reality for Nigeria until the fears and suspicions of other tribes, learnt in childhood could be displaced by mutual understanding and the confidence that is derived from it. To deal with this, recruitment to the courses was deliberately organized to provide a cross-section of regional and professional interests in each course. In the second place attention was given to the fairly generally accepted assumption that "Senior Service" status was commensurate with a large salary, a flashy car, contempt for physical and manual work, and indifference to the needs and interests of others.

To encourage a sense of social responsibility and to create an awareness of moral obligation towards others as a consequence of holding responsible positions carrying high social status members of the courses always take part in a piece of social welfare work or community development. An example of the kind of work undertaken is the Wovea resettlement scheme.

For many generations the villagers of Wovea had lived on a barren rocky island without water and without land for cultivation, entirely dependent upon fishing as their means of livelihood. To help the community to develop a more satisfactory way of life with prospects of progress, the Government provided land on the mainland for some of the younger men to establish a new settlement. The students at the Man O' War Training Centre assisted in clearing the land, designing the layout of the village, building a model house as a pattern of construction at the same time, up to date and inexpensive, and helped in laying the foundations of the houses. Other community development projects provided similar opportunities for practice in translating a sense of community responsibility into reality.

The project had many critics. It was seen by some to be another example of the way the British tried to make Nigerians into Englishmen. To others it was a waste of time and money to take

pen-pushers from their jobs and make them undergo a period of
training which included much physical exercise and labourers'
work only to return them to their pen-pushing where they
would forget all about it. If there was money to be spent, it was
argued, why not spend it on sending them abroad for further
training to advance them in their own careers.

Despite the criticisms, in the course of ten years some 3600
young men and women passed through the Centre, and when
the former trust territory of Southern Cameroon was united
with the Cameroon Republic in 1961, the Federal Government
of Nigeria thought well enough of the scheme to provide a new
site for the Centre at the Kurra Falls, about 50 miles from Jos in
Northern Nigeria. The scheme was re-named, the Citizenship
and Leadership Training Centre under a Federal Law enacted
on 1 October 1960. The first course organized at the new Centre
was a three-week schoolboys' expedition for boys from secondary
schools and the Nigerian Military School. The range of courses
has been extended to consist of: open courses—available to any
suitably sponsored candidate; senior courses—open to men
holding senior appointments; teachers' courses—mainly for
students from teacher training centres; women's courses, schoolboys' expeditions, extension courses—for groups from specific
organizations or institutions; community development courses;
and educational camps for youth clubs and younger children. In
addition a touring team is envisaged which will concentrate on
courses for post-secondary school boys to fill in the period of
waiting after their final examinations and the publication of
results, projects for teachers, administrators in training, and
university students, is envisaged.

The Citizenship and Leadership Centre started as a replica of
a training project developed in Britain to meet one specific need.
In Nigeria it has been adapted and modified to serve a variety of
related interests, and in the course of that adaptation two problems of considerable importance to the unity and the social
development of the nation have been given explicit recognition.
One is the need to break down barriers of fear and suspicion

which reflect the inter-tribal antagonisms of the past; and the other is the need to develop a strong sense of social obligation in the minds of those people fortunate enough to rise to posts of authority and responsibility in the community.

The second project which it is proposed to examine briefly, is the establishment at Ayetoro of a demonstration comprehensive school under the joint auspices of the Government of Western Nigeria and the United States Operations Mission to Nigeria.

The authors of the project* have attempted to combine in the school educational elements of American, British and Swedish approaches to secondary education and to adapt the result to "Nigerian reality". Yet their first proposal flies in the face of present Nigerian reality, in that they state: "There will be no entrance examination . . . admission being granted to all graduates of the elementary schools which will form its basis." With the disparity between the numbers of pupils completing their primary schooling and the number of places available for secondary education, one small group of primary schools assured of places for all their products in one particular secondary school whilst everywhere else there has to be competitive selection, is hardly to be described as an exercise in reality or a demonstration of the democratic principles that *all* Nigerian children should have a chance of at least entering the secondary school.

The school programme has been designed on the assumption that pupils might leave at three different points. During the first two years all pupils pursue a common curriculum, with the proviso that French or Additional English are alternatives in the second year. In the third year a number of elective subjects are introduced, the obligatory subjects being described as practical English, practical calculations, practical science, with separate courses for boys and girls, elementary economics, elementary sociology and Nigerian problems. The elective subjects are divided into four groups, pre-agricultural, pre-vocational, pre-commercial and home economics.

* A. Skapski and B. Somade, *A Demonstration Comprehensive School for Western Nigeria* (1961).

The third-year course of study is visualized as falling into two categories, a practical third form with electives named in the previous paragraph and a general third form pursuing general studies with elective biases and providing the necessary preparation for the General Certificate of Education, and for the few leading on to sixth-form studies which are intended to be a synthesis of the British sixth form and "the first two years of American University College studies".

In drafting the project, the authors have recognized that at the appropriate end-points pupils will need to obtain acceptable qualifications, and have assumed that for those who pursue the vocational studies, the end point will be the City and Guilds Certificate, for those who choose the general education biases, the General Certificate of Education at the ordinary level, and for those who carry on into the sixth form, the General Certificate of Education at the advanced level.

In pursuing the objective of providing for the educational needs and potentialities of every child the scheme presupposes the provision of adequate counselling and the acceptance of the counselling. The assumption is made that only the "upper" 50 per cent of the pupils should be given the opportunity to stay in school after the first level to pursue vocational and general education. "If the student insists on continuing in school and if he is a 'border-line' case, we feel that he should be given a chance and be admitted on the condition that he will show adequate achievement during the next half-year of study." It is also assumed, on the basis of Swedish experience, that half the students on their own initiative will choose practical subjects.

These assumptions are open to question. The prizes in life to be gained by continuing a general rather than a vocational education at the present time in Nigeria are so great that there is likely to be considerably greater pressure from pupils and their parents for them to pursue general rather than vocational studies. The pattern of life and industry in Sweden is very different from that in Nigeria, suppositions based upon social behaviour in the former are unlikely to prove safe guides in the latter.

The suggestions put forward for the proposed syllabuses at the three levels and in the different groups have been planned with a view to the need to modernize the secondary school curriculum, and to take advantage of work that has been done elsewhere, particularly in the United States, in mathematics and science. In what might be described as the Humanities considerable imagination has been shown. But nowhere are there signs of appreciation of the gap that exists between the more advanced thinking in educational circles and that displayed by the generality of the community.

The project as envisaged by its authors represents an attempt to synthesize advanced thinking and practice in three very different countries as an experiment in Nigeria. Assuming that the staff, half at least of which will have been recruited from outside Nigeria on short contracts, can weld themselves together into a team capable of interpreting the ideas of the authors, the school is still likely to prove an exotic institution. As such, given time, it will undoubtedly have its own peculiar contribution to make to education in Nigeria, but as at present conceived it is hardly likely to provide a pattern to be generally emulated.

One problem which occurs in every country where there is considerable dependence upon expatriate workers, is how to provide educational facilities for their children. Some of them are able to attend local schools, but for many this is not possible, or if it is, it has to be at the expense of places that ought to be available to local children. Apart from the question of providing facilities at all, because the expatriates come from different countries, there is the problem of relating the content of the education to that of the home educational system. In Nigeria, an attempt has recently been begun to deal with this matter by the opening of an International Secondary School at Ibadan University.*

The school is modelled in some respects on Gordonstoun School in Scotland, which was founded by Kurt Hahn on a broadly based curriculum with considerable emphasis upon character training.

* A. Taylor, The international secondary school at University College, Ibadan, *West African Journal of Education*, **7** (1) (1963) 5–6.

At Ibadan instruction is given in a common core of studies leading to Nigerian, British and American qualifications for admission to further studies, and, as at Gordonstoun, considerable emphasis is being placed upon the all-round development of the individual, self-discipline within the context of the school organization and the development of sound habits of work.

By organizing the pupils in small classes on the basis of comparability of age, ability, interests and future educational and vocational prospects, it is hoped to be able to cater for the diversity of need and interests which is inevitable in a school population of which the local element is likely to be the most stable, and at the same time a minority of the enrolment.

The core subjects are English (Language and Literature), History, Geography, Mathematics, General Science or a selection of sciences taken from the elective subjects, Music, Art and Physical Education. The elective subjects are, Modern Languages, Classics, Physics, Chemistry, Biology, Rural Science and Home Economics. In addition provision is made for hobby classes including, Woodwork, Metalwork, Mechanical Activities, Gardening, Elementary Animal Husbandry and Needlework. Following the pattern at Gordonstoun expeditions, excursions and service groups are to be organized, and pupils will be able to qualify for Duke of Edinburgh awards by meeting the requirements of physical ability, demonstration of public service, individual discipline and responsibility.

The school's first headmaster was formerly second master at Gordonstoun, and arrangements have been made for young Nigerian staff, as appointed, to receive training experience at Gordonstoun. Steps are being taken to establish a similar relationship with other international schools.

The school is co-educational with provision for both day and boarding pupils. The first phase of development has been made possible by grants from USAID, the Ford Foundation, and the Western Region Government. Although the school is the property of Ibadan University, the School's Board of Governors includes in its membership local Nigerians and representatives of the various foreign sectors of the local community. The Headmaster is a member of the staff of the University of Ibadan Institute of Education, and in that capacity can be expected to contribute to the development of educational thought and practice in Nigeria from the experience gained in the development of the school. The school charges fees which are assessed upon the principle of the school being self-supporting financially. The Western Region Government provides a number of scholarships for local children.

In this project we have an example of an attempt to deal with a problem of limited concern to Nigeria as a whole, but which, by the manner it is being approached, is bringing into the education system a number of new features. The links that the school has with the Institute of Education are such that though not a demonstration school in the conventional sense of the term it is likely to have some impact upon the outlook of those responsible for secondary education. In its attempt to cater for children who come from diverse educational and cultural backgrounds and for the most part are likely to return to them, the school may have much to offer to educational thinking generally in the flexibility of the teaching methods used and the content of the subject-matter taught. Whilst the immediate impact of its international character upon thought and attitudes is not likely to be great, over a period of time it may well prove to be of considerable importance.

One factor likely to limit the significance of this school and of the comprehensive school referred to previously is that of money. By virtue of the external financial aid both for capital and recurrent expenditure these schools are bound to be exceptional in some respects. Neither the government nor the grant-aided schools of the voluntary agencies will be able to emulate these schools in all that they attempt. Even so the experience gained by modification and adaptation should prove of general value.

The fourth project to note is one in which Nigerians are working with Africans from East, West and Central Africa under the leadership of Educational Services Incorporated. The latter organization is a non-profit body established to undertake curriculum studies in the United States. It came into being through the activities of a group of scientists and mathematicians at the Massachusetts Institute of Technology. As their first objective, they chose to design a new physics course for the high schools in the United States, appropriate to the mid-twentieth century. In 1961, the same group of people together with a number of scholars from other American universities met with a group of African educationists to learn something of the educational problems of Africa and to discover in what ways American experience gained in curriculum studies might be of use in Africa. One outcome of this study was the setting up of a Mathematics Workshop as part of an African education programme. Demonstration seminars were organized, first at Accra in Ghana; then at Ibadan in Nigeria; followed in July–August 1962 by a workshop at Entebbe, Uganda, "to lay out guide lines for mathematics curricula, designed for African use, and covering the entire school period from the primary years through the sixth form, and to prepare materials for experimental use in schools, or for teacher training". At the first workshop, which was attended by university staff, representatives of ministries of education, training college staff and classroom teachers, material was prepared for experiment in the first year of the primary school and the first year of the secondary school. In addition a series of objective tests, for experimental use in selected schools in East and West Africa, in algebra, arithmetic and geometry parallel in content but differing in design from the traditional School Leaving Certificate Examination papers was also prepared.

Whilst the preparation of materials was based upon curriculum materials that had been developed through a number of programmes being pursued in the United States, the intention was not to obtain the adoption of the American programmes but to bring to bear upon the African education scene the fruits of the experience gained in exploring the New Mathematics in the United States.

At a second workshop, also held at Entebbe in 1963, besides reviewing the experience gained by teachers who had tried out the materials designed in the previous year, new materials were prepared including the first drafting of guide material for teachers.

Several features of the project deserve comment. In the first place, instead of a new syllabus being devised by a committee or, as not infrequently had been the experience in Africa, by one person, the syllabus and materials for teaching it have been worked out jointly by classroom teachers, university teachers and educational administrators working together. Secondly, the syllabus and materials are being tested in the classroom and revised in the light of the experience gained. Thirdly, it is recognized that the teacher in service must be catered for if the new syllabuses are to prove successful in the classroom. Such an approach calls for resources and a time schedule that have not previously been possible in Nigeria, and the full implications of which have yet to be realized.

But there is another consideration to be noted and that is:

> Africa has been rather fortunate to have the Entebbe Workshops. We are in the forefront of experiments going on in various parts of the world in the teaching of the "New Mathematics". In the past our ideas for the development of education came to us through Britain; and although developments are being made in Great Britain at the present time, it would normally have taken several years for these ideas to reach the English-speaking countries in Africa. Now we do not need to lag behind; we can move forward together.*

That comment, made by Mr. J. O. Oyelese of the Ibadan University Mathematics Department, who has been a participant in the project from its initiation, underlines an emotional factor that is as important to note as are the educational features of the project. Much will have to be done after the project is completed before the schools receive the fruits of the work. What has been clearly demonstrated up to this point is the feasibility of a method of working which not only makes up-to-date material acceptable alike to the classroom teacher and the university specialist, but also requires active co-operation between various members of different sectors of the education system that has not previously occurred.

* J. O. Oyelese, The second Entebbe mathematics workshop, summer 1963, *E.S.I. Quarterly Report*, winter–spring, 1964, pp. 93–101.

The four projects which have been described and commented upon represent new developments concerned with specific educational issues. A very different kind of project of a much more general nature which may have long-term consequences for education in Nigeria was the Comparative Education Seminar organized in 1962 by USAID (Nigeria) under a project agreement with the Federal Government of Nigeria and the University of Nigeria. Sixteen Nigerian educators and education officials spent three weeks in Sweden, three weeks in France and four weeks in the United States, examining the educational systems of these countries in order to gain some insight into educational trends generally recognized as progressive that might be relevant to Nigerian interests.

In each country visited the group was briefed by prominent local educators about the education system, visits were then made to schools, and plenary sessions were held to review experience as interpreted by the sub-groups organized on the basis of the participants' special interests.

The recommendations and suggestion made in the report of the seminar do not add anything new to what has been said many times before. Indeed, they could as well have been made by the group sitting together somewhere in Nigeria and culling the major reports and plans for education in Nigeria that have been produced over the past forty years. One defect in the programme is noted by Dr. Skapski in his introduction when he comments: "It is my personal feeling that it would have been better, from the purely professional point of view, to give the Nigerians more time to get in touch with the life in the foreign countries whose educational systems they were studying."* If this had been done, the group might have shown greater understanding of the relationship between the provision of education and the social and economic factors influencing that provision in each country visited. Even so, the fact that the seminar resulted in a group of Nigerian educationists reiterating educational objectives pre-

* Ministry of Education Eastern Nigeria, *Report of the Comparative Education Seminar* (Official Document No. 21 of 1963), pp. 3 and 10.

viously defined by expatriates and visiting specialists, and doing so out of their own observations is a matter of considerable value. Also of some importance is the fact that the group consisted of representatives of each of the regional ministries as well as of the Federal Ministry and of the universities. The keynote of the Seminar report is an attempt "to focus attention on those aspects which upon adaptation might fit into our own situation and to help to improve the educational systems now existing in all parts of Nigeria".*

The projects which have been described in the foregoing paragraphs each illustrate in their different ways how borrowing from the experience of others is a major feature of the development of education in Nigeria at the present time. They also are indicative of the slowness of the process of natural growth in education. Borrowing is not necessarily to be deplored, but it does call for the exercise of judgement by both the borrowers and the lenders. Both should be able to assess clearly the needs of the Nigerian situation and the relevance to it of experience and practice developed elsewhere in circumstances that rarely are exactly parallel. In this respect, the development of the Citizenship and Leadership Training Centre out of what was essentially an alien method transplanted and modified in the light of local interests deserves the attention of all educationists in Nigeria and in other countries similarly placed. Equally deserving of attention is the methodology of the mathematics project which makes it possible for Nigerians to move forward with educationists from countries which enjoy older and more richly endowed education systems. The two school projects described, in their different ways, are likely to raise issues in secondary education of content and method and possibly throw new light upon the solution of them. The assessment of their worth will call for patient observation and sympathetic understanding of their objectives in the context of changing social circumstances.

* Ministry of Education Eastern Nigeria, *Report of the Comparative Education Seminar* (Official Document No. 21 of 1963), pp. 3 and 10,

CHAPTER 9

ORGANIZATION, PLANNING AND THE FUTURE

IN THE foregoing pages a description has been presented of the development of education in Nigeria, a development which can be paralleled in all the countries which can be classified as being traditional or transitional in character to use the categories defined by W. W. Rostow, or, underdeveloped, partially developed, and semi-advanced, to use the groupings suggested by F. Harbison and C. A. Myers.*

The first period of development of education was initiated by the individual efforts of missionaries in Nigeria. In other countries, too, the first steps were, more often than not, also taken by the missionaries, but in some cases a government official, acting in a semi-official or private capacity, took the first steps to introduce Western education, and in some instances the initiative was taken by a private trader or other philanthropically minded person or group of persons. Governments as such took no responsibility for providing education as part of an official policy. Government participation in education first took the form of giving limited financial aid to voluntary agencies, then moved on to providing some educational services to groups which, for one reason or another, were left outside the missionary effort, such as the Moslem element of the population, or to providing advanced and vocational education which was necessary in the public interest but beyond the resources or the interest of the missionary organizations.

* W. W. Rostow, *The Stages of Economic Growth* (C.U.P. 1960). F. Harbison and C. A. Myers, *Education, Manpower and Economic Growth* (McGraw-Hill, 1964).

The formal recognition of education as the responsibility of Government, first of all only in terms of the general control of education and, later, in terms of total responsibility as a national service, began in the latter part of the nineteenth century. In Nigeria this phase of development was completed by 1940, in other countries similarly placed it was not until the mid twenties of the present century that government responsibility was recognized, but by 1950 most governments had taken over total responsibility, whilst still accepting the assistance of the missionary and church organizations as well as those of other voluntary agencies in the providing of schools and training teachers.

The first significant development in the post-1945 period was the adoption of the policy of primary education for all children of the appropriate age as a major plank in the platform of the local political parties pressing for independence. With the taking of political independence free primary education was initiated in Nigeria, first, in the Western Region, secondly, in the Eastern Region, and finally in the Northern Region. This step revealed one of the prime problems, still a major difficulty, the lack of accurate data about the population. In the Western Region of Nigeria it was estimated that the number of children who would register for admission in the first class of the primary school would be 170,000. In the event 400,000 did so. The situation in most of the underdeveloped countries is the same. In consequence it has proved exceedingly difficult, and in most cases impossible, to provide accurate projections of the numbers of pupils to be taught, the numbers of teachers to be trained, the number of classrooms to be built, the numbers of books required and the amount of equipment to be purchased. In every instance, the estimates have been sadly short of the actual figures. In the Eastern Region of Nigeria the situation was anticipated by the civil servants, but they were overruled for political reasons; eventually, for lack of funds, the payment of salaries of teachers was delayed and some were not paid at all. As a result the teachers went on strike, and Government had to modify its policy in respect of charging school fees as part of the way of meeting the costs of running the schools.

One other difficulty which arose from the decision to make primary education free was the inadequacy of local government machinery to cope with the responsibility of meeting certain charges in respect of the maintenance and equipment of the primary schools. In some instances, the local government employees were not capable of carrying out their duties, in other instances, the local population was unable to, or did not wish to pay the additional local taxes which were intended to replace school fees as the source of income for the schools.

These features of the first attempts to provide universal primary education have been repeated in many other countries. They serve to underline the need for adequate statistical services and for the general education of the community about the kinds of demands that development of educational facilities will make upon them.

One other consequence of the decision to provide free primary education for all is now beginning to trouble the Government of Nigeria. The majority of the people assume that because in the past children on completing primary school education could expect to find wage earning employment they can continue to do so. The disparity is so great between the numbers of children now leaving the primary schools, having completed their primary education, and the number of places available for those who wish to pursue post-primary education together with the numbers who can obtain wage earning employment, that the crowding of unemployed persons into the larger urban centres and the social problems that follow has become a matter of serious import.

Reference has been made to one attempt at dealing with this problem, namely the land settlement scheme, but the cost of this is such that only a small number of the school leavers can be catered for in this fashion.

This particular experience shows the difficulties that can arise where the planned development has been inadequately related to all the interacting forces in the situation. The political reasons for embarking upon a programme of primary education for all were paramount, the economic considerations were ignored. In this respect greater wisdom was shown in former French West Africa, where the principle of free primary education for all was accepted as a matter of regional policy, but the timing of its application was left to local authorities. The readiness of the population to participate in the extension of education, in most countries varies from district to district, and recognition of this fact is a consideration that should enter into the planning. Phased extension of facilities in relation to regional readiness to respond could ease the immediate financial burden of the implementation of policy.

The lesson to be learnt from Nigerian experience in respect of the extension of primary education is, that in the same way as economic development is a process which extends in range from communities only slightly removed from a subsistence economy to communities with the elaborate social and economic structure of the Western nations, so is educational development a continuum with an appropriate policy relevant to each stage. This lesson is defined by implication in the educational pyramid postulated in the Report of the Commission on Post-School Certificate and Higher Education in Nigeria.

> In deciding on the pattern of education we have been guided by the following principles: (i) It must produce enough children with post-secondary education to satisfy the nation's needs for high-level manpower. (ii) It must be properly balanced as between primary, secondary and post-secondary education. (iii) It must narrow the gap between educational opportunities in the North and the South, without producing an unbalanced education system in the North.*

It must be remembered that the Commission was considering the educational pyramid in so far as it serves to support the higher education needs of the country for the next twenty years. The difference between the small numbers they visualize going on to secondary education in the Eastern and Western regions and in Lagos, 1000 completing primary school (according to the commitment of universal primary education), of these seventy should enter secondary grammar schools; suggests that the

* *Investment in Education* (Federal Ministry of Education, Lagos, 1960), p. 10.

planning and development of primary education should be much
more closely related to the economics of the country as they
affect the products of the primary school system.

Primary education is in all essentials a process of mass
enlightenment.

> This enables the masses of the people to participate in economic activity.
> And it opens men's minds as they can be opened in no other way, to new
> methods and new techniques. Apart from its cultural role, popular
> literacy is a highly efficient thing. Needless to say, it is also the mainspring
> of popular aspiration. As such it adds strongly to the desire for develop-
> ment. If the development is to depend on popular participation, then
> there must be a system of popular rewards. There can be no effective
> advance if the masses of the people do not participate; man is not so
> constituted that he will bend his best energies for the enrichment of some-
> one else. As literacy is economically efficient so is social justice.*

The truth of this has been borne out already in Nigeria, where
the general strike of June 1964 represented the response of the
labouring classes, essentially the product of the primary school
system, to the failure of the Government to match the rewards
of the labouring classes with those obtained by the very small
élite fraction of the community.

When we turn to the secondary education scene, we find that
the traditions of the former colonial powers are strongly en-
trenched in the secondary schools. Whilst this is a matter that has
been subject to much criticism, the relevance of the form of education provided was a good deal closer to the realities of local
needs in the past than the critics are generally willing to admit.
Until *political* independence, economic and political circumstances set a premium upon an education in the humanities. That
there is need to develop variety in the kinds of secondary education has since been recognized, and some attempts are being made
to produce suitable alternative forms of secondary education.

There are, however, serious difficulties confronting the educational planners. In the first place, the populace, in so far as it has
an opinion in this matter, is wedded to the traditional patterns,
particularly as they represent the mode of qualification for
admission to the universities. Secondly, the attempts to provide

* J. K. Galbraith, *Economic Development in Perspective* (O.U.P., 1962), p. 13.

technical and vocational training have not gained the interest of many people, and the status of the technician in Nigerian society is not yet such as to attract young men and women in any considerable numbers. A third difficulty arises from the fact that the majority of Nigerian secondary school teachers are themselves the product of a system that honoured the traditional grammar school curriculum and, as elsewhere, it is extremely difficult for any but the exceptional individual to divorce himself from his past values. Added to this factor, the rest of the secondary school staff consist of expatriate teachers the majority of whom are on short-term appointments and are mostly inexperienced; on both these grounds are they unlikely to make any significant changes in the content or of the methods of teaching in the secondary schools.

There is, however, one line of development which could make a major contribution in this field of educational development, that is the team approach to the design of the mathematics syllabuses that has already been referred to in Chapter 7. The combination of local teachers, university teachers, administrators and external agencies committed to the design and testing of new material, drawing upon resources in other countries, emulating but not imitating developments elsewhere, could compensate for the weaknesses in the staffing of the secondary schools and ensure the continuity of action which has up to the present largely been lacking in the attempts to revise the curriculum.

The crucial factor for success in such development is the existence of understanding co-operation between all concerned. This is not easy to attain. The outside specialist will invariably be an exceptional kind of person, and those very qualities which contributed to his achievements in his own country may well prevent him from comprehending the problems to be faced elsewhere. The local participants are not necessarily free to adapt new material and new techniques quite as easily as they might wish. They have to operate within the existing system. The examination requirements may not permit of radical changes in the content of a subject or in its treatment, and examination success is of paramount importance not only to the pupils but often also to the reputation of the teachers. However ready the administrators may be to encourage experiment, they are inhibited by political, financial and organizational considerations.

For example, the educational administrator may well be persuaded of the exceptional value of the language laboratory, and yet a proposal from some outside body to provide a laboratory as part of a pilot project may prove very embarrassing. If the project is successful, the administrator is faced with the problem of deciding whether to recommend general adoption on educational grounds or to turn down the proved new technique because of the financial implications. Providing language laboratories for all the secondary schools and training or retraining of teachers to use them will not be inexpensive. It often is easier to give acceptance in principle, but to avoid actual commitment to action, than to risk the complications of deciding who shall have the privilege of carrying out the pilot project, and what to do if the project is successful. If curriculum revision is to be carried out successfully it will be necessary to have an established policy based upon continuous assessment of the educational needs in relation to the objectives of social and economic development. It will also be necessary to harness all the resources available to the execution of the policy. In none of the present experiments in secondary education in Nigeria can it be claimed that these prerequisites have been satisfied. In so far as secondary education is concerned, experience elsewhere is the same.

In the field of technical and adult education in Nigeria, the present situation is one of inadequate facilities and of difficulty in formulating suitable policies. Except for the large industrial and commercial organizations, it has so far proved impossible in practice to obtain from the private sectors of industry and commerce the kind of information that is essential to planned development of education. The major organizations, both government and private, still depend largely upon on-the-job-training to provide their own skilled manpower needs. The attempt to establish middle-level skilled technical manpower through the Nigerian

College of Arts, Science and Technology foundered, partly because overmuch emphasis was laid in the initial stages on the development of teaching at levels parallel to university teaching; partly because the planning of courses was carried out with little consultation with industry and commerce, and with virtually no reference to economic planning; and, partly because socially and economically the prospects did not attract the products of the secondary schools.

Adult education has made comparatively little growth, partly, because the majority of the politicians have been committed to a policy of maximum effort in the extension and development of formal education, and partly because satisfactory forms of adult education for the present conditions have yet to be devised. The strength of the political indifference to adult education is all the more difficult to understand because the value of a literate community had been emphasized in Nigeria by individual civil servants earlier than in most countries, and some of the district and regional efforts at adult education have been very successful. In view of the importance of the immediate improvement in the contribution to the skilled needs that could be obtained by the better education of adults, the causes of this indifference on the part of the politicians should be examined. It may be that it reflects the dominance in the Federal and Regional parliaments of members who were formerly teachers, or it may be a reflection of the strength of the belief of the people in formal education as the keystone to individual advance. For many people, the education of their children is the means of safeguarding both the future of their children and of themselves.

At the university level, extra-mural activities in Nigeria were started in a way that showed an imaginative attempt to meet local conditions. But this failed, partly because of the lack of financial resources and partly because of political suspicion. There followed a period of activity which reverted closely to the tradition of extra-mural studies in Britain. The latest developments suggest that university effort in extra-mural activities are likely to be much more narrowly directed towards providing

specific help to individuals who wishing to pursue university
studies in order to obtain degree qualifications, cannot gain
admission for lack of the qualifications for admission, or for lack
of money to support themselves and pay the fees, or because
there are no vacancies for them.

The pattern of adult education as it has been developed in
Nigeria suggests that the question of choosing what proportion of
support should be given to the formal and the non-formal sectors
of education requires considerably more attention than it has
been given hitherto. Apart from the prejudices of local politicians
and administrators in this respect, it is of some interest to note
that adult education has attracted little attention from sources of
bilateral aid, and that the greatest efforts to stimulate its development have been made by UNESCO.

It is not inappropriate in this respect to make reference to some
remarks made by Mr. A. Deleon, as the representative of the
Director-General of UNESCO at the Regional Conference on
the Planning and Organization of Literacy Programmes in
Africa, held at Abidjan, Ivory Coast, March 1964:

> We are here . . . because more than 700 million men and women—almost
> half of the world's adult population—are at present cut off by illiteracy
> from effective access to the sources of science and education, and because,
> out of the 700 million, at least 105 million live in Africa.
>
> There are those who believe that the only effective remedy—the only
> necessary remedy—for widespread illiteracy is universal primary schooling.
> Teach the children and let the older generation of illiterates die out. This
> is not only a denial of the universal right to education, it is also a short-
> sighted policy . . . if this policy were to be adopted—generations of illiterate
> adults in Africa would be a burden on the national income of their
> countries for many years and that they must be given the means to work
> more efficiently, to earn more, and to contribute to raising their national
> standards of living. A mass of illiterate adults will—in the nature of things
> —hinder the economic, social, cultural and even political progress of
> countries that have recently gained their independence. Even those who
> maintain that education should be given to children alone have found
> that in many countries children returning from school to illiterate com-
> munities rapidly regress into illiteracy. . . .
>
> The elimination of illiteracy, however, is not merely an integral and
> inseparable part of continuing and general education; it is closely linked
> with all the other aspects of contemporary African life. Literacy cannot be
> achieved in isolation. It is not an end in itself. On the one hand, illiteracy

is the result of under-development, and on the other, lack of economic and financial means impedes the struggle against illiteracy and the effort in favour of adult education. These are the reasons which incline us all to associate education for literacy with the creation of individual and collective motivations, and with the existence of opportunities open to new literates. Without adequate motivation and real opportunity, literacy training—and education in general cannot attain their goals. This is why our Conference must give special emphasis to the establishment of inter-relations between economic development, social emancipation, the elimination of unemployment, the modernization of agriculture, indus-trialization, literacy and continuing education, and also to planning the strategy of the campaign against illiteracy—a strategy that will vary with each country and with different circumstances, need and possibilities.*

Reflection upon Nigerian experience underlines the need to regard literacy and adult education as an integral part of the educational programme of any country. That this has not been so in the past is due, in part, to the fact that different facets of adult education have been regarded as the responsibility of particular agencies and there has been no machinery either to co-ordinate efforts or even more importantly, to plan on an integrated basis the activities of the individual agencies in the total social and economic context of development.

In university education, Nigerian institutions are based upon patterns developed in Britain and the United States with stan-dards of entry and graduation of the same status as those in the countries they have imitated. The relevance to the interests of the country of the content of the courses provided and of the standards that have been accepted are now in question, partly because of the cost of university education and partly because of increasing appreciation of the need for large numbers of people with university training of a general nature compared with the rela-tively small numbers of people required with specialized qualifications.

The establishment of universities under both federal and regional auspices with different entry standards has raised the issue of comparability of standards of qualifications. The limita-

* UNESCO, *Final Report of the Regional Conference on the Planning and Organization of Literacy Programmes in Africa* (UNESCO, Paris, 1964).

tions on the resources available for the universities has raised the question of concentration of facilities and the avoidance of duplication of effort in several institutions. The problem of sharing the cost of financing university education between federal and regional resources and between the public and the private purse has also become important. These internal issues have resulted in the establishment of national machinery to ensure the maximum efficiency in the development and the exploitation of the resources available. It has proved impossible to provide free education for all. The provision of scholarships and bursaries by the governments in addition to providing the money for all the basic costs is limited. It is likely, that increasing numbers of students will have to pay their own fees. This could ease the burden on the governments. But the extent of failure of many of the present students admitted as private fee payers to meet their bills has forced consideration of other means of ensuring that the fee income of the universities is safeguarded.

It has been pointed out that if the Nigerian governments directed all the Nigerian students at present attending universities overseas on government grant to Nigerian universities in order to take their first degrees, the indebtedness of private students to the Nigerian universities would be eliminated. As an alternative procedure it has been proposed that a system of loans with security for repayment after the graduate has taken up employment would not only prevent the accumulation of bad debts by the universities, but would also ensure that the individual who benefits personally from his university education repays the country for the advantage it has bestowed upon him.

These are issues that many of the other low-income countries have to face. The fact that many students go overseas for their first degree qualifications may jeopardize the effective growth of the local universities and may lead to inefficient use of the resources that have been established. In some cases the opportunities to go overseas have been provided by outside agencies. In so far as the individuals return trained and equipped to contribute skill to the country this may be well counted an asset, but whether this is in fact the most efficient way in which such aid could be given, remains an open question.

The idea of repayable loans is, of course, not a new one, but in Nigeria, it will for many people be a novel idea because at the university level it has increasingly been assumed that Government ought to provide the education free. The repayment of loans will require some kind of bonding system. Teachers trained in missionary training colleges in Nigeria are not unfamiliar with the idea, but in the past experience in implementing penalties when the bond is broken has not been very successful. A study of the attitudes of the people in respect of economic development, however, may show ways in which such a form of investment might be encouraged. Any efficient way of spreading the immediate burden of the cost of university education so that a significant element of the cost is later borne by the beneficiaries is to be welcomed as much in other low income countries as it is in Nigeria.

The organization and administration of education directly reflects the historical development from a colonial dependency to the status of political independence, the colonial administration for education being converted into a ministerial organization, with a Cabinet Minister responsible for policy to the people through Parliament. Thereby the dual function of a Director of Education as the designer of policy and as the chief executive officer responsible for the implementation of policy was abandoned. A civil servant as Permanent Secretary to the Ministry became responsible for overall administration, and another officer, as Chief Education Officer, exercised professional direction of the education programme. The administrative and inspectoral duties formerly carried out simultaneously by educational officers at provincial and district levels were separated, and an inspectorate was established as a separate professional cadre within the ministry.

Federalization involved a further process of reorganization. Each Region, East, West and North, now has its own Ministry of Education, so the need for consultative and co-ordinating

machinery is more apparent, particularly in respect of university
education and external aid. As has already been mentioned,
this has led to the establishment of a National Universities
Commission and the All-Nigeria Academic Council. Whilst the
former body is responsible for examining the financial needs of
the universities in relation to the planned balanced development
to meet national needs, the latter is intended to maintain the
academic standards. The membership of the National Universities Commission is representative of the national interests of
the country and it has its own secretariat. The membership of
the All-Nigeria Academic Council is drawn from the academic
boards of the universities and is responsible for the standard of
the qualifying examinations in the universities.

The division of responsibility between the federal and the
regional ministries is essentially a political matter. For, under
the Constitution, education outside the Federal territory of
Lagos is a function of the regional governments, except for higher
education which is a concurrent activity while legislation in
regard to certain existing institutions is the exclusive responsibility of the Federal Government. The plan for educational
development for the period 1961–70, however, is so vast, that
in addition to calling upon the people of Nigeria to treble their
present efforts for education, a large increase in external aid will
be needed if the plan is to be carried out successfully.

The Federal Government has accepted the responsibility for
co-ordinating the efforts of the regional ministries in matters of
common concern by organizing meetings of ministers, of permanent secretaries and of professional educational officials. In
addition, arrangements have been made to establish a co-
ordinating body specially charged with the co-ordination of
applications for external aid and with the supervision in Nigeria
of schemes of technical assistance for education. Representatives
of each of the regional and the federal governments serve on the
body. Despite the existence of this machinery the approach to
the seeking of external aid is far from clear. In a White Paper
on the proposals of the National Universities Commission pub-

lished in 1964, it was proposed that grants from the Federal Government to the universities should be reduced by whatever funds the universities had been able to attract from external sources. Whilst the intention to save federal funds in this way appeared on the face of things to be reasonable, the fact that such action would prevent the universities seeking to supplement their budget for research and development purposes from outside sources was overlooked. When the weakness in the proposal was pointed out the White Paper was withdrawn.

One reason for the error lies in ignorance of the way in which universities work and also of the nature of their work. In particular, little is understood of the relation between teaching and research in the universities. In this respect Nigeria is much like many of the other countries for whom the university is a post-war achievement in the local provision for education. Unfortunately, the universities are rarely the best expositors of their duties and of the ways in which they operate. With experience both governments and universities will establish a better understanding of each others responsibilities and relationships. The steps which have been taken in Nigeria to provide machinery to ensure satisfactory working relations between Government and the universities should ensure a proper balance between the development of education in that sector and the development in the other sectors of formal education. It should also afford a model for other countries at a similar level of educational development.

An educational system, however well planned, is not an entity in itself. There is no political situation more likely to cause difficulties for the Government than one in which the economy of the country is not capable of absorbing the products of the system at the various points at which they leave it. As has already been pointed out, this is already a problem with regard to primary school leavers. In respect of the high level manpower training, a National Manpower Board has been established and steps have been taken to make a register of people training both in Nigeria and overseas. The next step will be to continue the statistical examination of the different skill requirements of the

country in relation to the existing and planned economic development programme. Linked with this is the need for increased
sophistication in the analysis of the agricultural background of
the different groups, of the sectoral distributions of the population as between industry, services and agriculture. The need
for so doing has been recognized. Mr. S. O. Awokoya, the Federal
Adviser and Permanent Secretary for Education, commented
upon this problem in a conference on educational planning held
in Berlin in 1963.

> We are gradually discovering some of the costly mistakes we have made
> during the last five years. In Western Nigeria a big effort was made to
> start farm institutes in order to absorb as many primary school leavers who
> tend to flock into the cities. But these institutes have been over capitalized
> and expenditure exceeding £1,000 per child has been undertaken—a
> rate of capitalization that appears to be beyond our present economic
> capacity. Further, great hopes were entertained about the capacity for
> employment at the oil undertakings in Eastern Nigeria. Later it was
> found that a modern oil industry depends more upon equipment which
> will require little attention. We are, therefore facing the problem of labour
> intensive and capital intensive industries for which no easy solution can be
> evolved. In recent considerations of the problem, the view has been
> expressed that a special commission must be established consisting of those
> who promote economic development and manpower development, so
> that the greatest amount of correlation might be achieved alike in their
> plans and in their implementation. Only then can the ultimate purposes
> be achieved—to deploy trained personnel into good employment.*

In this respect the educational planners are dependent upon
the extent to which the manpower needs have been identified
and a closer analysis than has hitherto been possible of the trends
likely to develop in skill requirements.

The Ashby Commission drew attention to the regional disparity between the numbers of people being educated in the
Northern Region and the numbers being educated in the other
regions. Whilst this is explained as the outcome of past policy
and the indifference of the Moslem community towards Western
education, there has been no systematic study of the extent to

* S. O. Awokoya, *Educational Planning in Nigeria, International Conference on
Educational Planning in Developing Countries* (Deutsche Stiftung Fur Entwick-
lungslander, Berlin, 1963), pp. 15–16.

which the social and cultural factors inhibiting educational demand in the north can be identified. It therefore does not appear to be possible, at the present time, to determine to what extent the educational attainment of the parents, their social and economic standing, are likely to impede or accelerate the demand for education. In the same way, in the Eastern and Western regions, there has been no systemic study of the social demand for education in relation to economic aspirations. For this reason, past efforts at preventing the "drift from the land" have not been successful. In fact it will not be possible to devise a policy for directing the social demand for education unless there is precise knowledge of the factors that create the demand. Yet planned development implies the directing of the social demand for education into economically useful channels.

Nigeria is rapidly accumulating educational experience. As the numbers of educated parents increase this is likely to lead to increased demands for education. Present planning for educational development will almost certainly prove inadequate unless some measure of the cumulative rate of increase of demand can be established.

Crucial to the development of education and to the production of the appropriate numbers of skilled persons is the supply of trained teachers. In Nigeria this has been dealt with by increasing the numbers and the size of the training colleges, the provision of new courses for experienced non-graduate teachers, building advanced training colleges with assistance from UNESCO, and by organizing vacation courses staffed by teachers and teacher trainers supplied for short periods from the United Kingdom. That the results have not been entirely satisfactory is due to the fact that certain issues in planning and maintaining the supply of teachers have not been given the systematic attention they deserve. The minimum and the desirable levels of qualification of teachers for different types of pupil in the education system has been assumed to be those which already exist. The attempts to bring teachers already in service up to date have been limited to a series of *ad hoc* courses unrelated to either the expanding rate of knowledge or the development of new techniques. Furthermore, comparatively few teachers have been able to benefit from these courses and there has been no provision for systematic follow-up. Little attention, as yet, has been given to the relative attractiveness of teaching compared with other occupations, and the tension between the demand for people in the economic and administrative sector and for teachers to train more skilled people has not been the subject of systematic analysis. Another aspect of the teacher problem which has received little attention, and certainly has not been considered as a matter of policy, is the extent to which all skilled people might be potential part-time teachers and what particular teaching skills might be given them in order to make the best use of their services wherever possible. Up to the present, use has been made only of a limited number of wives in this way. These are matters which call for investigation rather than speculation. In this respect Nigeria is much like the other low-income countries in that the approach to the supply of teachers has been in terms of assumed targets based upon the numbers of pupils expected at the different levels and traditional concepts of the appropriate teacher–pupil ratio. Research into this problem linked with research into teaching techniques might provide better guidance in establishing the demand for teachers and the demand for teaching. The latter is a distinction of some importance when it comes to planning development of teacher training.

A continuing source of anxiety in providing education in Nigeria is the cost of school buildings and equipment. Mr. S. Awokoya, the Permanent Secretary and Adviser to the Federal Ministry, described the situation in the following terms:

> Years ago, Nigerian schools were easy to build because they were simple structures intended to protect teachers and pupils from sun and rain. Some of these simple village schools remain till today after lasting for over forty years. They harmonize with the other buildings in the village and are functionally useful. The old desk and benches were designed without due regard to the physical comfort of the pupils. This kind of error is fortunately a thing of the past. A few lessons can, however, still be learnt from these village schools. It is clear to us in Nigeria today that

if we are to achieve universality in primary education, our economic means allow us to embark only on a school building programme that provides good shelter in an adequate number of class-rooms with utilitarian equipment without endeavouring modern sophistication; otherwise, the education of many children will be sacrificed for architectural elegance. A lot can also be done by the use of local building materials and standardization of design and equipment. Such an arrangement was followed in the Western Region in 1954 when the primary school class-rooms were built and equipped at the very low cost of £200 per class-room. In Lagos, today, the average class-room costs £1,700.... Experiment in the cheapening of the class-room unit for primary education is an urgent requirement if universality is to be obtained without financial catastrophy.*

Despite this appreciation of the problem, and it is a much more serious problem at the secondary school and teacher-training college level, the establishment of school building units has not yet proved possible. In terms of equipment, attention at the moment is focused upon the supply of textbooks. Steps are being taken to develop co-operation between the established textbook publishers, almost entirely United Kingdom in origin with the potential local resources for production, and also to develop textbook production under government auspices. But this development has not yet proceeded very far. The danger here is that anxiety to save on the cost of books may result in the setting up of local textbook units within the ministries of education without adequate skilled editorial, technical and administrative staff to ensure satisfactory production. Only if the problem is seen as one of establishing a new industry and that it is planned in those terms, is this particular burden likely to be effectively reduced. In this as in so many other aspects of the development of education in Nigeria there must for some time to come be some dependence upon external aid.

In planning the development of education in Nigeria, the place of the voluntary agencies will need to be given special consideration. The continuing importance of the part they play was underlined recently, by Dr. the Hon. S. D. Onabamiro, Minister of Education, Western Region, when he addressed the 4th Synod of the Diocese of Ibadan, and appealed for the help

* *Ibid.*, p. 7.

of the Synod in the realization of the Government's new educational programmes. He said:

> I believe the solution lies in the contribution which the Voluntary Agencies can make in the development of our education. . . . (1) Closer supervision of primary school expenditure by Voluntary Agencies on behalf of government. (2) The introduction by the Voluntary Agencies of a system of merging small classes and small schools within their respective organizations. If this were done, Voluntary Agencies would be saving for government a sum of more than half a million pounds a year. . . . (3) The reintroduction of education subscriptions in their various churches.*

This comment echoes the kind of appeal that might have been made any time during the last fifty years in Nigeria. It is all the more significant a pointer to the continuing importance of the voluntary agencies in that today the Nigerian governments pay in full the salaries of the teachers employed in the voluntary agency schools whilst management of the schools including the hiring and firing of the teachers remains with the voluntary agencies. One important reason for their continuing importance lies in the fact that even if the governments of the Federation wished to take over the complete control of the schools they could not do so for the lack of the managerial experience which the Voluntary Agencies possess. Furthermore, as was pointed out in the Report on the Review of the Educational System in Eastern Nigeria, the voluntary agencies "succeeded more than the Regional Government or the Local Authorities in arousing local interest in education and in raising funds from local communities, for educational purposes".† J. O. Anowi suggests that

> The older Voluntary Agencies, that is to say, the missionary organizations, use their experience in the field of education in the country, their intimate knowledge of the people and in general their prestige, without financial profit, in order to wield influence in the shaping of the educational policy of the country. Even where the government has decided on a policy, it has to court the support of the Voluntary Agencies to make it a success.‡

* Quoted in *Nigerian Education*, edited O. Ikejiani (Longmans, Nigeria, 1964), p. 51.
† *Report on the Review of the Educational System of Eastern Nigeria* (Ministry of Education, Official Document, No. 19 or 1962), p. 47.
‡ J. O. Anowi, The role and function of voluntary agencies in Nigerian education, in *Nigerian Education*, edited O. Ikejiani (Longmans, Nigeria, 1964), p. 52.

Even so, the increasing participation of the Government in the direct management of the schools, colleges and the universities represents a change of emphasis which will continue and will eventually force more specific attention in planning to be given to the role of the voluntary agencies in education.

A much more pertinent question at the present time, however, is how to establish and relate external aid to educational planning in such a way as will ensure proper use of the funds available. Up to the present time external aid for education in Nigeria has been provided in terms of specific individual projects, varying from the help given by the Carnegie Corporation to financing the Commission on Higher Education, and assisting in the provision of a unit in the Federal Ministry to co-ordinate aid, to grants to individual schools and scholarships from a variety of agencies, national and philanthropic. UNESCO aid has varied from the providing of experts to the establishing of Advanced Training Colleges. Various countries have given special assistance for higher education, and many foundations have given assistance for research projects.

Valuable as these contributions have been, there does not appear to be a policy, unless it is a policy to obtain what you can from whoever you can. As in other low-income countries Nigeria needs to find out how to make better informed choices in the allocation of resources, both internal and external, to the different sectors of the education system. Until this is possible the choice between accepting or rejecting offers of aid will not be possible except in terms of hunches.

Related to this subject is the need for the educational planners to be well acquainted with the significance of the other charges that must be met from the country's budget and of the fiscal capacity of the community to support all those charges. Much external aid is intended "to prime the pump" on the assumption that recurrent costs will be met from local resources in the near future. In most cases, the relation between capital and recurrent costs of educational enterprises initiated with external aid has not been properly calculated. As a result the country finds itself in great difficulty in maintaining the impetus that has been given to the expansion of education.

So long as the public educational system has to assume responsibility for training in those skills which are scarce because the labour force has not been able to build up a critical mass of skilled persons able to sustain and reproduce itself, and of producing additional workers by on-the-job training, Nigeria will have to depend to a considerable extent upon external aid both in the provision of manpower and in the provision of training. Sometimes external aid is provided to give overseas training of a technical and vocational character at levels above those immediately required locally. The result is that expensively trained professional workers are employed on tasks which in developed countries would be performed by lower-grade technicians. Planning the integration of this aid into the national economy will involve questions of local, national and international standards and qualifications which are subject to the influence of such factors as prestige and professional status and these might be at odds with immediate needs for specific kinds of service.

These are among the many considerations that have arisen out of the current attempt to develop education in a planned fashion in order to accelerate the economic and social development of Nigeria. They show that more detailed examination is required of the needs and objectives of the educational programme by both Nigerian and donor agencies than has been possible up to the present.

In this respect the criteria used by the International Bank for Reconstruction and Development in appraising loan applications for loans for educational facilities can provide a guide to research, the results of which could guide the planning of further educational development in Nigeria as elsewhere. These criteria are:

(1) Educational standard, including organization, management, content and product.
(2) Manpower considerations as related to economic and demographic factors.
(3) Fiscal standards in operating the educational system.

(4) Construction and procurement standards.

In the main, these are considerations that are new to educational thinking. But they are matters of prime importance to the continued development of education in Nigeria if it is to be carried forward in such a way as will ensure the fulfilling of the aspirations of the people.

The major emphasis in the planning of the development of education in Nigeria since independence has been with reference to the production of a supply of men and women with the knowledge and the skills necessary to carry out the work which will raise Nigeria from being one of the lesser developed countries into one capable of taking a full part in the world affairs. Only by becoming strong economically, independent in politics, and culturally creative in its own right, will Nigeria be able to contribute to world affairs as an equal with all other nations. But the economic and technological needs of the nation are only one aspect of the educational needs of the nation. Whilst the national purpose of education is to equip the people to bring about the modernization of Nigeria in the quickest possible time, it is also concerned with serving the individual.

> It is thus incumbent upon the government of Nigeria to assess its educational programmes in terms not only of how well they serve national schemes, but also how well they serve the individuals themselves. It is never only the nation's political, social and economic development that is sought it is also an improved quality of individual social participation, economic betterment, and political contribution. . . . The aim is to produce a nation that will be both modern and free: no lesser goal will suffice. It is only within this framework that education for economic growth, education for civic and political development, and education for social and personal integrity have democratic meaning.*

The intellectual climate at present dominating the thinking about education in Nigeria, as in most of the underdeveloped countries, is in large measure the outgrowth of the new emphasis upon economics. But it has its roots in traditions powerfully influenced by Judaic–Greek concepts of the nature of the

* J. O. Anowi, The role and function of voluntary agencies in Nigerian education, in *Nigerian Education*, edited O. Ikejiani (Longmans, Nigeria, 1964), p. 52.

individual as interpreted by the evangelical and liberal traditions
of Britain.

> It will be increasingly subject to other influences of other cultures, including
> Islam and Communism as well as the continuing influence of the Western
> world. But above all, it will reflect the dynamism of the people of Nigeria,
> already forging anew its values, borrowing and modifying the experience
> and knowledge of other peoples in terms of their own genius.*

Despite the elementary state of knowledge of the techniques of
planning educational development in relation to political, social
and economic progress, enough has been achieved to assure the
future growth of the educational resources in the national and the
individual interests of Nigeria.

* J. W. Hanson, The nation's educational purpose, in *Nigerian Education*,
edited O' Ikejiani (Longmans, Nigeria, 1964), p. 21.

FEDERAL MINISTRY OF EDUCATION: HEADQUARTERS ORGANIZATION

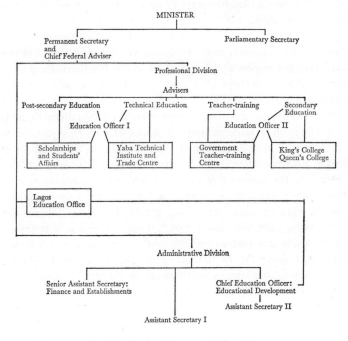

Note: Executive organizations are enclosed in panels.

APPENDIX 2

THE CONTROL OF EDUCATION

THE control of education in Nigeria is divided between the federal and the regional governments. There are differences in the details of nomenclature used and the structure of organization of the different authorities vary in detail, but the essential framework is the same. The regional ministries control primary and secondary education in each of their own regions. Greater use is made of the voluntary agencies in the Western, Eastern and the Mid-Western region and Lagos than in the Northern Region in the provision, management and supervision of schools; and voluntary agencies also have a greater share in the advisory and policy making aspects of education outside the Northern Region.

At the ministerial headquarters, a similar pattern of organization exists. A permanent Secretary is responsible to the Minister for the administration of the Ministry. A Chief Education Officer supervises the day-to-day activities assisted by administrative and professional officers responsible for primary, secondary and teacher-training and inspection, except in Lagos where the organizations are too small for such detailed division of responsibility. There is a certain amount of fluidity of the actual duties taken by officers. At the time of writing, in the Western Region, for instance, the duties of Permanent Secretary and Chief Inspector are undertaken by the same officer.

The government secondary grammar schools in the Western Region are usually controlled direct from headquarters. Voluntary agency grammar schools are controlled by boards of governors which consist of representatives of the agencies and of the Government, and are responsible to the regional headquarters of the voluntary agency organizations. Secondary modern schools in the Western Region are controlled by local education authorities. In the Northern Region the provincial secondary schools are controlled by boards of governors or by advisory bodies responsible in the first instance to the Native Administrations and the provincial education officers. Regional government education officers are posted to these schools to assist in the staffing of them. Technical institutes and trade training centres are controlled directly from headquarters.

Teacher training colleges are controlled by the appropriate authority, Central Government, Regional Government, local education authority, Native Administration, or voluntary agency according to whom proprietorship is vested. In the case of the voluntary agencies, as a general rule, they have either boards of governors, boards of trustees, or managers, who are responsible to the regional headquarters of the agencies.

Government exercises considerable control over the teacher-training colleges by prescription of the syllabuses and by controlling the qualifying examinations as well as through the financial provision of grants.

Control over the voluntary agency secondary schools is largely exercised by Government through the system of grants-in-aid.

Whilst there is some liaison between government ministries in respect of technical education as well as between the ministries of education, business and industrial organizations, the control of technical education is entirely within the ministries of education.

Each of the regional ministries have separate branches or divisions responsible for inspection duties. In the Western Region there are staff inspectors at headquarters in charge of the separate sectors of education, with inspectors and assistants in the provinces. In the Northern Region there are senior inspectors for teacher-training and secondary education at headquarters, and there are regional inspectors in each of the provinces. In the Eastern Region there are headquarters inspectors for secondary education, teacher-training and technical education. In each region there is a chief inspector in charge of the section or division.

Relations between the ministries of education and the West African Examinations Council are controlled by official membership of the council committees and by financial controls.

Control of the universities is vested in individual councils on which the governments have representation in addition to the financial controls exercised through the National Universities Commission. Inter-university affairs are controlled through the All-Nigeria Academic Council.

THE EDUCATIONAL LADDER

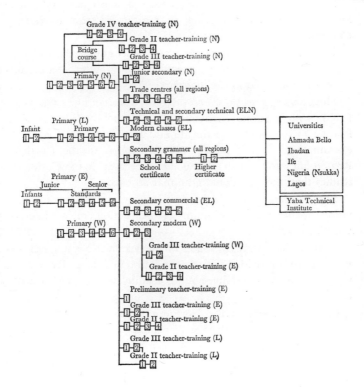

NOTES TO APPENDIX 3

The *bridge course* is a one-year course for Grade IV teachers in the Northern Region and some uncertificated teachers to help them qualify for admission to Grade III teacher-training colleges.

The *junior secondary schools* in the Northern Region provide a two-year secondary grammar school course.

The *modern classes* in the Eastern Region and in Lagos provide a two-year course with a strong practical bias.

The *preliminary teacher-training* course is a preparatory course for candidates for admission to Grade III teacher-training colleges.

The *primary education* courses vary in length in the different regions from six to eight years with varying patterns of organizations as indicated in the diagram.

The *secondary grammar schools* provide courses of five or six years length with a strong academic bias, in the English tradition, leading to the School Certificate and Higher School Certificate examinations. The *Provincial secondary schools* of the Northern Region fall into this category though they provide more practical studies than the traditional grammar schools.

The *secondary commercial schools* are characterized by the provision within the curriculum of instruction in commercial vocational subjects.

In the *secondary modern schools* of the Western Region a three-year course is provided with a strong practical bias. There are a variety of teacher-training courses leading to Teacher's Certificates.

Grade IV courses in the Northern Region are of *four* years' duration after the fourth year of primary education. Previously these courses were known as *vernacular training courses*.

Grade III courses, two or three years in length, lead to the Teacher's Elementary Certificate (Grade III).

Grade II courses provided in the Eastern Region are of four years' length for candidates who have completed their primary education. In the Western Region, candidates are admitted to these courses after completing two years in a secondary modern school. In the Northern Region admission is gained after completing two years in a secondary grammar school. In this grade is also included a two-year course for holders of Grade III certificates and for candidates who have completed the secondary grammar school course. Teachers holding these qualifications can be admitted to the examination leading to the award of the Teacher's Higher Elementary Certificate.

Trained experienced teachers with suitable qualifications can obtain admission to courses at the universities for specialist training of an advanced nature. These courses are normally one year in length.

Technical training is provided through part-time and full-time courses varying in length according to the subject.

Trade centres, provide courses of training in trades such as cabinet making, plumbing, painting and decorating. In addition, certain industrial and commercial firms provide technical in-service training together with organized courses full-time and sandwich fashion.

Admission to secondary education and teacher-training is obtained by success in selection examinations. Admission to post-secondary education is gained by combination of appropriate qualifications obtained at the end of secondary education and entrance examinations.

Tuition fees are payable in all forms of post-primary education but there is varying provision of scholarships and bursaries made by the regional and federal authorities for a large number of candidates for courses.

SELECT GENERAL BIBLIOGRAPHY

1. BIBLIOGRAPHICAL REFERENCES

COUCH, M., *Education in Africa: a select bibliography*, Part I, University of London Institute of Education, London, 1962.

HARRIS, J., *Books about Nigeria:* Ibadan University Press, Ibadan, 1959.

IBADAN UNIVERSITY LIBRARY, *Nigerian Publications 1950: a list of works received under the Publications Ordinance*. Since 1955 publications from outside Nigeria have been included in the list.

2. NIGERIAN GEOGRAPHY, HISTORY, ECONOMICS, POLITICS

BUCHANAN, K. M., and PUGH, J. C., *Land and Peoples of Nigeria*, University of London Press, London, 1955.

BURNS, SIR ALAN, *History of Nigeria*, George Allen & Unwin, London, 6th edition (8th impression), 1963.

COLEMAN, JAMES S., *Nigeria Background to Nationalism*, University of California Press, Berkeley and Los Angeles, 1958.

FEDERAL GOVERNMENT OF NIGERIA, *Annual Abstract of Statistics*, 1960, Federal Office of Statistics, Lagos, 1960.

FEDERAL MINISTRY OF ECONOMIC DEVELOPMENT, *National Development Plan, 1962–1968*, Federation of Nigeria, Lagos, 1962.

Handbook of Commerce and Industry, Federal Ministry of Information, Lagos, 1962.

INTERNATIONAL BANK FOR RECONSTRUCTION AND DEVELOPMENT, *The Economic Development of Nigeria*, Johns Hopkins Press, Baltimore, 1955.

NATIONAL ECONOMIC COUNCIL OF NIGERIA, *Economic Survey of Nigeria*, National Council, Lagos, 1959.

3. EDUCATION

Educational Development 1961–1970, Sessional Paper No. 3 of 1961, Federal Printing Division, Lagos, 1961.

HILLIARD, F. H., *A Short History of Education in British West Africa*, Thomas Nelson & Sons, Edinburgh, 1957.

IKEJIANI, O. (Editor), *Nigerian Education*, Longmans, Nigeria, 1964.

Investment in Education, Report of the Commission on Post-School Certificate Higher Education in Nigeria, Federal Ministry of Education, Lagos, 1960.

LEWIS, L. J., *Educational Policy and Practice in British Tropical Areas*, Thomas Nelson & Sons, Edinburgh, 1955.

MELLANBY, K., *The Birth of Nigeria's University*, Methuen, London, 1958.

OLDMAN, H., *The Administration of Primary Education*, Government Printer, Kaduna, 1961.

OLUMBO, A. FERGUSON, J., *The Emergent University*, Longmans, London, 1960.

Report of the Commission on Higher Education in West Africa, Cmd. 6655, HMSO, London, 1945.

SAUNDERS, J. T., *University College, Ibadan*, CUP, Cambridge, 1960.